The Gentle Art of Pottering
Sailing the P15

By

Dave Bacon

Dedication

This book is dedicated to Dave Dolan, who served as my crew and good friend from our earliest years.

Acknowledgement

Books don't get written without the help of others. I had no idea when I first started out, the size of the project I was taking on. The fact is, it wasn't me taking on the book, it was the other way around. It became a journey of discovery, learning, and finally one of a great fulfillment .

This book would never have been written without the help and encouragement of my mentor, Richard Herman. Following his wise counsel and advice I achieved beyond what I thought possible.

Both Don and Judy Person gave their full support to the project. Don did all of the pictures which was no easy task. Judy pitched in and volunteered to take on the challenge of proof reading.

Larry Brown donated the picture for the cover taken by Bettina Brown.

This picture perfectly conveys the messing about Potter philosophy.

To write a book, you must have a quiet comfortable place to work. In the little house we share, my wife, Judy, made this possible by adjusting her activities around my work schedule, always placing her fresh cut roses at my work space.

Last but not least, it was Gretchen Ricker who took all the bits and pieces of our combined efforts putting them together to make the book you now hold in your hand. She's done an excellent job and is responsible for much of the book's success.

To all these people just mentioned and others who played smaller parts, I thank you, and am indebted for your support and effort.

Table of Contents

Introduction

No matter how much you enjoy life, there are times when you just need to take a break. If you find relief down by the water, then pottering about in a small sailboat may be just the answer. Pottering, using the English definition just means to mess about. So what does pottering about in a small boat have to do with art? Again, it's a matter of definitions, and Webster's defines art as the skill acquired by experience, study, or observation.

If you're attracted to the charm of sailing small craft, then you'll find that taking your skills to the next level is all part of the natural process of sailing. Many think of this type of activity as an art form, and this is exactly what "The Gentle Art of Pottering" is all about.

Let's just take this idea one step further. You're walking along the shore, and have wandered out onto a float where small boats are docked. You see one in particular that stands out among the others. It's as though this particular boat had been painted in a picture, and then was built by someone. It's a work of art, or at least someone's idea of what a small boat should be.

While standing there in contemplation you begin to feel somehow this moment in time is exceptional, one of those moments that are never forgotten. Without further thought, you take one step forward and find yourself aboard this little craft. No decision was made about doing this, it just happened, as though the boat itself had invited you aboard.

"What if", you think, "I were captain of such a craft as this. What could I do with it? Where could I go?" Suddenly you begin to find yourself looking at a whole new world. Just taking that single step into a small boat now includes the idea of learning how to sail your own boat. This is just the first step into what will become "The Gentle Art of Pottering." Perhaps it's just a coincidence, but the boat you've been standing in, is in fact, a West Wight Potter Fifteen.

These Potters, known as P15's, are an excellent choice for serving your needs on the water. And if you've a mind to, you can take a P15 and create your own version of what the art of pottering is all about.

There are several important reasons for writing about P15's. Many Potter sailers out there are isolated in areas where little sailing exists. Even when using the internet, they're left with limited information which is often inferior to direct contact with experienced Potter sailers. It's the reason for writing this book. Its goal is to simply explain all the information needed for managing and successfully sailing a Potter.

If you sail a P15 now, this book will show you how to make your sailing experience much more worthwhile and rewarding. Even if you sail a boat other than a Potter you'll still find a wealth of important information. After all, small boats have much in common. The tone of this book, I'm sure, will inspire all of you to get out there and sail your boats better than you ever have before. It's not

intended to teach basic sailing. If you don't know how to sail, you should take sailing lessons.

The organization of this book will lead the reader through common activities that sailors do. You'll start with the basics of how to buy a Potter and setting up your P15 for day sailing. From there you'll move on to learn more effective cruising and racing skills. Also discussed are modifications to your Potter that will make your boat faster and easier to sail. Helmsman ship and sail trim skills will be coordinated with Potter modifications that will boost your sailing and boat speed.   Each topic, will be explained in simple terms, and then expanded on as needed. You'll read examples, modeling how good sailing is done. Readers will be provided with a common sense point of view, and conservative outlook for sailing their Potters. Using the information contained in this book will allow you to sail safely and effectively, while looking forward to many more pleasant adventures on the water.

   Happy Pottering!

Foreword

I've owned a lot of boats over the years, all of them built of wood. For me, wooden boats feel and sail differently. They also have a stronger sense of tradition. Of course, this aesthetic way of thinking is a personal issue. For me to get around that, it took some out of the box thinking to come up with the idea of buying a Potter.

Just by chance, I purchased a boating magazine called the "Small Craft Advisor". One of the articles that caught my eye was a review of the P15. I had seen them sailing at various times. They're fifteen feet long, with a beam of five and a half fleet, and draw three feet of water. These little boats, rigged as sloops, carry about ninety square feet of sail and are quite seaworthy for their size. Potters also use small Honda outboards to bring them home when the wind fails. Being simple to rig, they're mostly used for day sailing, but have two long bunks below for overnight cruising.

To me, they looked like reasonable boats, very straight forward and honest. Without its cabin, the Potter appeared similar to the v bottomed plywood boats we would sail as kids.

In a later copy of the same magazine, there was mention of the coming Cruiser Challenge in Monterey, California. As it was only two hours away by car, I decided to check it out. During the Challenge, I watched the boats and met many people who sailed Potters. They were open, friendly, and enthusiastic about their boats and club activities. I felt welcome right from the start.

Often on Wednesdays, while sailing on a retired friends boat, we would see Potters sailing on the Oakland Estuary near San Francisco. We would always close the distance just to watch them sail. I liked the cut of their mainsails, they were different. It was fun watching them move over the water like a little armada. I found the idea of Potters sailing in company an attractive one.

Later, that spring there was a boat show on the estuary. A P15 was on display, so I went to see it. As I walked toward the display tent, I couldn't help but notice all the Potters out on the water being sailed by their owners in support of the boat's builder, International Marine. The Potter representative took the time to point out the boats best features, and answer all of my questions. Then he left me alone with the boat so I could really look it over.

I was impressed with the quality of the boat which was so much better than the earlier models I'd seen. I liked the idea of a cabin on such a small boat. Previously, I had cruised in an open boat, but found the exposure to sun and wind overwhelming. Once again, the idea of overnight cruises began to hold some attraction for me.

"You're going to buy a Potter aren't you?" the returning salesman said,

Taken by surprise, I agreed.

However, it was several months before I arrived at the Potter factory in Southern California, and ordered my new boat. Being retired, I felt that a new boat would be the best choice. I didn't see many opportunities to own other boats in the future, so this one had to be a keeper. It would be a retirement gift from my wife.

After nine years, I continue to cruise and race with the Northern California Potter Yachters, enjoying some of the best sailing possible in P15's.

As I look back now on all the sailing I've done, I remember the first three Potter skippers I sailed with. They were my mentors, modeling the best ways to rig and sail Potters. Those three skippers were wise in the ways of small boats, and on to something good. I'm just glad to have been a part of that and share so many great sailing experiences with them.

Adopting a Potter

What makes a P15 special?   Let's start with the boat's name," West Wight Potter". These little boats were designed by Stanley Smith, and built on the western end of the Isle of Wight. The word 'wight' means stalwart or valiant. To potter, as I have said before, is an English term used for messing about. Potters have lived up to their name by safely completing several long voyages. While not recommended, they've been sailed from Mexico to Hawaii, and Seattle to Ketchikan, as well as across the North Sea.

Potters came on the American boating scene sometime in the late sixties when an American bought a wooden West Wight Potter and had it shipped to the United States. He set up a company using his Potter as a mold, and began producing P14's in fiberglass. Sometime later the Potter design was upgraded with a new sail plan and self bailing cockpit becoming the P15's we know today.

Because Potters are micro-cruisers, they have small cabins which offer many advantages. When out sailing for the day the cabin provides a secure space for your lunch and other gear. If you decide to take a break and dine in a restaurant, or walk into town for a bit of exploring, you can use the boat's cabin to lock up what you don't take with you.

Because of their v bottoms and steel centerboards Potters are different from other micro-cruisers. This allows them to sit lower on their trailers having less wind resistance when being towed. It only takes six to ten inches of water to float a P15, which makes launching easier, even at difficult ramps. While sailing in shallow water the problem of running aground is easily solved by raising the centerboard.

Should you decide to beach your Potter for a picnic, it will sit nearly upright on the beach.

Adopting a Potter is a wise choice if you're looking for a small sailboat to use in sheltered waters. If you've just learned to sail, or have limited sailing experience the Potter works well as a trainer helping you to develop you're sailing skills. If you've been sailing for a longtime, but are choosing to downsize because of limited resources or physical limitations, the Potter is economical and easy to sail. In fact, many people who own Potters are retired and on fixed incomes. Joining a Potter club will provide group sailing activities and helpful support while you learn about your new boat.

Potters are very practical to own and use, which is why they're so popular.

The Value of a Potter

We all know the value of money, which is measured by the amount time it takes to collect it. Your Potter also has a value too. It's value is tied to the amount of time you spend sailing it while collecting new experiences along the way.

So what's it like to climb aboard a Potter and sail away? Although I can't invite you aboard my Potter at this moment, I can guide through a short early evening cruise.

It's a late fall afternoon as the Potter makes it's way down the estuary with a party of two. As friends, these two sailors have sailed together for over fifty years, and are completely at ease on the water. There's no particular plan or goal for this cruise, except to have a picnic supper while enjoying a getaway sail during the middle of the week. The day begins to takes on an amber glow while the boat makes its way down the estuary. Both the skipper and crew are enjoying the sail, while sharing past memories.

"Hey," remarked the skipper, "Remember when we were rammed by that sea lion?"

"Yeah," the crew said, "You said he was asleep while swimming, and I said, I believe you're right.

Then about a second later there was this terrific bang, and water flew everywhere."

"Well, no damage done," said the skipper laughing as they moved on to other topics.

The wind, somewhat fitful, now coming from the northwest, challenges the Potter crew to sail on cat's paws through the momentary calms. Both skipper and crew share the sailing, each taking their turn at the tiller when sitting on the lee side. Because the wind has grown lighter, many of the other boats began lowering sails. Their skippers have found this type of sailing too challenging for their larger, less responsive boats. Meanwhile, the Potter sails on, playing with the wind shifts, while searching here and there for the gentle breezes that the cat's paws bring.

Finally, the wind, what little there is of it, ceases altogether. The Potter slowly glides to a stop on a glassy surface colored by the last of the setting sun. The picnic supper is brought out and shared while enjoying the first of the evening. Night Herons fly along the shore searching for places to fish. Other birds begin to squabble over coveted roosting spots in the tree tops as they settle in for the coming night.

Swimming over to the Potter, a lone seagull with a strong sense of entitlement, and very little patience pecks several times at the Potter's hull. This of course brings much laughter from the crew. But supper is over, and the gull will have to do without, except for a few left over crumbs.

The sun, long since set, has been replaced by the first stars in the east. Now, an evening breeze sets in, and the silence is broken by the gentle rustle of sails as the Potter comes back to life and begins moving through the water again. The new breeze brings a chill, so jackets are brought up from the cabin to stave off any discomfort. The boat moves along now almost with out a sound. Just the flutter of telltales can be heard as they rattle gently against the sails. No one talks, savoring this moment to be treasured for later times, when life's demands must be met. Later, the wind dies, leaving the Potter sitting sideways to an opposing tide. A vote is taken, and it's decided to motor back to the launching ramp.

Now, just like the other boats before them, sails are lowered and lines and fenders are made ready for docking.

Both the skipper and crew agree that it's been a good sail. It has broken the tedium of the work week. Such is the pleasure that can be had from just a simple sail for a few hours.

A sailing cruise is pretty much the same as a day sail. However, it can be more challenging because you're out on the water longer. There's a greater chance that weather conditions may change. When they do, you must adjust to them in a timely fashion, making safe sailing choices.

"How would it be, if I were to go on a cruise? What would that be like?" You ask.

Far to the north, in a small waterfront town, a Potter skipper works in his garage, stowing all the gear necessary for a three day cruise. The plan is to launch at a local marina, sail across the bay into the river, and then onto a connecting slough, seeking a secluded anchorage by nightfall.

The next morning finds the blue Potter sailing along with good wind and tide.

"So far, I'm on schedule," thinks the skipper, "but I really need to take advantage of this tide. If I don't, my anchorage will dry out before I get there. Better crack on more sail," he thinks. (He loves the power that more sail provides.) But with a strong westerly breeze coming off a thick fog, he thinks better of it. Besides, there's still three full hours of flood before the tide turns. Such changes in wind and water conditions are what make cruising so appealing. You just never know how it's going to turn out. As it is, the wind slowly builds to twenty knots, forcing the skipper to tie in a reef. After all, the boat is out on a large bay, with no one around to help if anything goes wrong.

But then this experienced skipper thinks, "That's not the way cruising is done. You have no business out here if you have to be rescued! You must rescue yourself, before you really need to be rescued, that's real cruising."

8

After awhile, the day warms up as the fog burns off leaving calmer winds. While peeling off his heavy jacket, the skipper puts the shock cord on the tiller, keeping the boat steady. After putting his life vest back on, he checks the chart for his position and pulls out a small cooker from down below. Hot chili is planned for lunch, and must be started early. The solar cooker uses a small wok and is built from garage sale parts, secured in the cockpit so it can be used underway.

Now that the wind has eased, the reef is taken out, bringing the Potter back up to full speed again. Lunch comes and goes as the Potter pushes on with a foaming bow wave. Having crossed the bay, and now onto the river, she's making good time. By mid afternoon, the buoy leading into the slough is sighted. As it slides by, the skipper jibes over and sails into the slough lined with tules on both sides. The ebb has been running for sometime now, and the banks of the slough show several feet of mud. There's still quite a distance to go, but even though the boat has slowed some, the skipper isn't concerned as he pulls a drink from his cooler in the cockpit.

"It's just as well that we're moving slower", he thinks , "a fixed bridge is coming up, and I'll need the extra time to check for mast clearance before sailing under. The chart shows it's going to be close."

Sailing on, the skipper reminisces back to when all pleasure craft used this convenient slough before the bridge was built. Today, only smaller craft can use this slough without lowering their masts.

"Well, there it is," the skipper thinks as he sails around a bend on the slough. Just then a farmer drives up and stops his truck near the bridge. He's been watching the boat's sails over the tops of the tules and wants to see if the Potter will make it under the bridge. After a quick visual check and a tense moment, the Potter just slips under.

"Now that was close!", exclaims the skipper out loud, "It's a good thing I didn't have the wind pennant up there." He waves to the farmer still sitting in the truck as he passes by. About an hour later the Potter sails onto a smaller slough.

"No water skiers in here today," the skipper thinks. "It's too shallow." Sometime later the centerboard begins to bounce and the Potter comes to a slow stop.

"Well, that's it," thinks the skipper . "It's not unexpected, but a bit disappointing just the same. I would have liked to have sailed all the way in, but it's not to be. I think I can make it into the anchorage if I hurry." So the sails are hauled down and furled, the anchor is made ready and the motor is started. Both the rudder and centerboard are lifted. The Potter slowly moves ahead as the skipper guides the boat with the motor. After a short while the slough dead ends into a small pond lined with tules, just right for a small boat. The anchor is set and a stern line is taken to an old stump. As all is secured, the skipper settles back taking a break, just listening to the silence of it all.

A dying breeze rustles the tules, as the Redwing Blackbirds sing, and a cow calls in the distance. Supper is prepared as the sun sets, casting an orange glow on the clouds to the east. Now, flocks of

Redwing Blackbirds fly overhead calling as they go. The skipper, taking a moment from his cooking duties, looks up to admire the last of the sunset. Sensing the coming darkness, he hurries to complete his galley tasks. Glancing down, he notices that the water is gone, leaving the Potter sitting in a sea of mud. The tide is out, and will not return until the early hours of the morning. Awhile later, the skipper sits in the cockpit, leaning back against the cabin, watching a crescent moon slowly climb up over the tules into the night sky. Finishing his coffee, he begins thinking about other anchorages, considering the possibility of sailing to a new one he's been curious about.

"After all, I still have several days before I have to go back. Oh well, tomorrow is another day," he says to himself, as he slips down below climbing into his sleeping bag and sliding the hatch closed for the night.

These two sailing examples should give some insight into the value a Potter can provide. So, if you already own a Potter, get out there and sail it. A P15 is not very well suited for use as a garden tool shed,

12

or laundry hamper. Potters are destined for much finer things. Let it be your vehicle to experience great adventure, or quiet solitude. It's all up to you.

Maintenance

Good maintenance is essential to the seaworthiness of your boat, and the safety of it's crew. However, as important as it is, it doesn't have to be a lot of work. With the right attitude, maintenance is nothing more than just messing about with the boat. Keeping an open mind, and learning as you go, is all part of this process.

After every sail, inspect your Potter as you wash it down. This will allow you to see what needs to be done to keep your boat in good condition. Make sure that everything works. Lines should lead fair with a minimum of friction. Blocks and cam cleats should operate smoothly, and sails need to go up and down with minimal resistance. A Potter maintained at this level is usually sailed a lot and a pleasure to own.

One of the secrets of maintaining your Potter, is to keep up with the projects that need to be done. As you finish sailing for the day, make a list of repairs or upkeep you want to do. Prioritize the list, then do one project at a time. While working on the project, make it fun to do. This is easily done when allowing all the time necessary. Avoid self imposed deadlines that create stress and the need to cut corners, bringing poor results. Even if you don't know how to do a needed repair, it can still be fun. Net working with other experienced Potter sailors is a good first step and P15 sailors often do that.

After gathering information from a variety of sources, select the best solution. When doing the project, consider the skills that will be needed, and the tools on hand to complete the job. To be successful, first figure out a step by step process in logical order to complete the project. Focus completely on each step, before moving to the next. With each step carefully completed, your results will be something to be proud of.

It's important to know when a project is too technically difficult. To avoid the frustration of a poorly done job, get professional help. While paying the bill, just remember how much fun the Potter has given you, and will continue to do so over time.

Improvements

You'll probably want to make improvements to your Potter as you become more familiar with it. I've made many to my boat. Some were made just to fit my sailing style, while others were done to make the boat more comfortable and convenient to use.

Improvements are done differently than maintenance and require a different approach. When making an improvement, you're changing a system that controls a function of the boats operation. Using that line of thinking, you'll want to focus on the system that you're changing, plus any other systems used in tandem with it to achieve a given task, not just the particular item you want to change.

Let's take a look at a few systems that Potters have: reefing, halyards, and self steering. The goal of each of these systems is to run smoothly and be easy to operate. These systems are mostly independent of any other, but at times must work together to complete given sailing tasks such as reefing. This should be kept in mind to avoid mistakes when making any changes, because when systems fail to coordinate you're forced you to rethink your project.

A good example would be when reefing the mainsail. Three systems are needed to complete this task. You'll use a self steering system when sailing alone, and also both halyard and reefing systems located on the starboard side so you can work them together at the same time. Even though separate, it's important that all these systems work together quickly and smoothly to complete their tasks. Your safety counts on it.

If you don't have the experience to see how these systems work in various sailing situations, help is available. One of the best places to learn about systems is at Potter club events. There, you can talk to other skippers. Most will be glad to answer your questions, and show you what they have on their boats. It might be a good idea to bring a pencil and paper to take information, or draw diagrams or layouts. A cell phone with a camera can be helpful too. Also, International Marine at westwightpotter.com, is a good source for information and replacement parts.

Keep in mind that if your new system doesn't enhance the ease of sailing and rigging your Potter, then it's not worthwhile. In the long run you'll probably replace it with something easier to use.

Maintenance and Costs

The maintenance and costs of owning a small boat are considerably less than a larger one. The obvious reason is that there's less to maintain, and its systems are not as complex. Estimating the annual cost for maintaining a Potter would be difficult. Each skipper values his boat differently, depending on how much use he gets out of it. This will determine how much time and money he's willing to put back into the boats maintenance. Also, expenses will vary, depending on the Potters condition. It's important to keep all your maintenance expenses in your comfort zone or you won't enjoy the boat. The five skippers I polled, agreed that twenty to thirty-five dollars a month seemed like a reasonable amount to cover general maintenance.

As a skipper you have to use good judgement about what you want to maintain or replace. Replacing old sails will cost about eight hundred dollars or more. A new trailer or outboard motor will each cost about one thousand dollars. (These prices are estimates for the year 2012.) It's a good idea to keep this equipment well maintained to save on replacement costs. The good news is, you'll get to choose how, and when you spend your money.

Besides maintenance, there are other expenses you'll want to consider: insurance, storage, registration fees, property tax, and a license fee for your trailer. When it comes to taxes, each state will be different. However, don't let all this discourage you, remember, because you have a small boat all your expenses are less.

When considering insurance, your biggest risk might be when trailering to your destination. The cost of repairs from an accident could easily exceed the value of your boat. If you already have insurance, be careful when making a claim. Never assume that your insurance company will cover all the expenses. Your insurance will probably pay the agreed upon estimate from the boat yard, but if the yard exceeds it's own estimate, and they often do, the insurance company will not pay the difference. I've seen this happen before.

As you stand there upset about having to pay hundreds of dollars that you didn't anticipate, the yard foreman will calmly point out the fine print on the back of your signed contract. It will read something like this, "The owner agrees to pay at the hourly rate of one hundred, five dollars, plus all material costs, exceeding the original estimate." The money must come from somewhere, the yard foreman explains, and the responsibility falls on the owner.

However, insurance is a good thing, considering what it covers for two hundred dollars a year. All it takes is one serious mishap to make it worthwhile.

One of the many reasons for having a small boat is to cut back on storage costs. If you're counting on storing a Potter in your garage, make sure it fits. If you're unable to keep your Potter on your property, then you'll have to make other arrangements.

Dry storage for a P15 close to the water can cost about a hundred dollars a month. Of course prices vary, but it's always more expensive in the best sailing areas. Dry storage does have advantages. You don't have to trailer your Potter far. Because the boat is usually close to the launching ramp, you may be able to leave the mast standing and the boat partially rigged. When there's a launching fee, sometimes a discount can be arranged because you're already paying a storage fee.

Any boat you own will cost money to keep, but, as it's been said before, small boats cost less and give a bigger bang for the buck.

These charges do add up, but they're spread throughout the year. Most owners do their own maintenance, avoiding boat yards when possible; this helps to make small boat ownership more economical. Your best defense against the burden of boat ownership, is to sail your Potter as much as possible, and spend your boat money wisely.

Impressions

Evaluating a P15 comes down to collecting impressions over a period of time that add up to experience with the boat. Using that process, you can compare the best and worst that the Potter has to offer. This is how a boat's strengths and weaknesses are measured.

Given that approach, an experienced P15 skipper will find his Potter has excellent sailing characteristics. The strongest of these are predictability. The Potter, when pushed beyond it's limits, will become progressively more difficult to handle. As control is being lost, you'll feel it through the tiller. This provides a margin of safety, showing the skipper that changes need to be made to meet the challenging conditions. However, if the skipper continues to push his Potter beyond all reasonable limits, then he'll find himself clinging to a capsized boat. This would be true of any small centerboard boat.

When sailing a Potter, I find that when I have a moment of doubt about what's going to happen next, I'm not in control, and must begin to make adjustments for my personal safety and that of the boat.

Potters can be capsized for all the wrong reasons. My personal favorite, is when someone standing on the cabin top loses his balance just as a gust heels the boat and then falls into the cleated mainsail. This doesn't make a Potter unsafe, or even a bad boat. All boats have their limits as to what they can do and it's the skippers duty to be familiar with them. The skipper who blames his boat, when disaster strikes, is no better than the poor worker, who would blame his tools. He just isn't being realistic.

As you gain experience sailing your Potter, you'll come to know that you have many safe options to choose from when challenged by difficult weather. These will be discussed in a later chapter and none of those will include capsizing.

A P15 is one of the easiest boats to sail taking little physical effort. Each sail can be trimmed with one hand, leaving the other free to manage the tiller. When the boat is balanced, as it should be, the tiller is light in your hand, making steering easy.

As small as they are, Potters are quite comfortable. The metal rails around the cockpit add a feeling of security seldom found on other small boats. Over all, the Potter gives the impression of being fun to own. The P15 is quite versatile and does many things well. What follows are two examples of that from past experience when cruising.

While cruising Desolation Sound with our Potter fleet, we sailed five miles across the Sutil Channel close hauled on a starboard tack in increasing wind. Five Potters started, and as expected, all made the crossing safely. One was under motor only, two had reefed mainsails with their jibs on deck and motors running. The last two, under sail only, had jibs up and single reefs in their mainsails. Each skipper, within his skill level,managed his boat to the best of his abilities. After an hour of sailing we all arrived safely at Heriot Bay. We were glad to get in. Once there, the weather report for our area told of winds thirty-two to thirty-nine knots in the gusts, which turned out to be more than predicted earlier. We didn't choose to sail in those conditions, but sometimes you just get caught out in them when cruising.

A few years later, during a cruise in the Canadian Gulf Islands, we arrived early at Clam Bay an hour after low tide. The water in the channel was still too low for most of the boats in our fleet. The "Admiral", our cruise leader, rounded up the Potters and sent us into the channel.

"Go forth and discover," he said.

We were told the other boats, those with keels, would follow sometime later, when the water was deeper.

As the first Potter, I moved into the channel under power and was eventually forced to raise both my centerboard and rudder. As the channel narrowed, it became impossible to turn around. Continuing ahead, and steering with the motor, I began to feel that it was just a matter of time before grounding. Up ahead, several young people waded knee deep across the channel in front of me with buckets and shovels searching for clams. Still, I continued on, I had little choice. The mud at the steep edges of the channel walled in what water there was and began increasing in height until I could no longer see over the top. Looking ahead, the channel appeared to be a dead end. But still, I moved into this canyon of mud in what certainly seemed an impossible situation.

I couldn't help but imagine what this scene might look like to other people on shore, just a mast moving through a sea of mud, something like a submarine's periscope.

Arriving at the end of what I could see of the channel, once again I prepared myself for the mandatory grounding and long wait for the rising tide. Suddenly, the channel doglegged to the left around a muddy corner, leading to some distant trees. As I came closer, the mud begin to give way to a shadowy forest forming a canopy over the channel creating new concerns about mast clearance. The channel, now lined with large rocks narrowed even further leaving less than five feet on each side of the Potter. Up ahead, it slowly became brighter. Several people stood on the bank taking pictures of the boat just as the Potter broke out of the channel and into a very beautiful harbor.

What I thought was impossible, had been achieved. Although the cruise along the shallow channel took less than an hour, it had become a great small boat adventure never to be forgotten, thanks to my Potter.

Buying the Boat

We've all been told at one time or another that honesty is the best policy. This holds true when buying a boat. Being honest with yourself allows you to be clear about choosing the boat you need. Asking yourself questions, such as when and where you'll sail, and how much time and money you're willing to spend to do that, will help in your search to find a boat that best fits your needs.

The reason for asking those questions, is to develop a practical frame work that will keep your emotions in check during the boat selection process. Boats that are purchased for purely emotional reasons seldom work out in the long run, and can be stressful to own. Even though they don't fit your sailing needs or finances very well, you're still the proud owner. But after a few years, the pride of ownership wears, off leaving you with a boat that must be sold. Maintaining that kind of thinking over the years, will keep you in a continuous cycle of buying and selling boats that you've fixed up. This is a very expensive way to support your interest in sailing.

To avoid this endless cycle of boat ownership, stick to the plan you've developed for choosing a boat. Once you've located boats that are for sale within your defined frame work, you can feel free to use your emotions to select the one you like best. Balancing both the practical and emotional aspects of boat buying will allow you to own your boat successfully for a long time.

If you're a future Potter skipper, you'll need to first choose between a new or used boat. Each has it's advantages. If sailing is new to you, then it's always a good idea to have an experienced sailor along to help answer questions before you make any choices.

The new boat, although more expensive, allows you to choose exactly what you want. For example, according to the P15 catalogue, (2010) you'll have many choices to consider. You can choose between thirty-two colors ,and two hull options. There are twenty-three options for sails and rigging. You also have three interior options and eighteen for the exterior. The electric options include fifteen choices. Also, there are several motor options.

As I remember, when I was buying my boat, the more I looked at the options on the list, the more I wanted. Be careful, it's very easy to purchase more than you need.

The used boat, although limited in it's choices, has other advantages. If you're new to sailing and not sure if you'll like it, then a used boat is your best choice. The used boat will cost less than the price of a new one. (Think cars here.) If you find that sailing isn't for you, then you can sell the Potter for about what you paid for it. Often inexperienced sailors have accidents, such as running into things, while learning to sail. Used boats often have suffered some wear and tear already, making a collision with your recent purchase not nearly as traumatic as it might be with a new Potter.

After thinking about the advantages of new and used boats, it's time to decide which is best for you. If it's the new boat, you'll have some research to do regarding choices. You can contact International

Marine at westwightpotter.com. If you've chosen the used boat, then it's time to start shopping.

Looking at other Potters is an education, and should be done by buyers of both new and used boats. This will help you understand how Potters are equipped. Usually, each one is set up differently to suit the needs of it's skipper. If you can, travel to as many Potter events as possible. When you see something you like, put it on the list and use your cell phone to take a picture of it.

If you decide to buy a new boat, be clear about the options you want before you order it. If possible, make an appointment and go to the factory. Sometimes there are new Potters that have not been delivered. It's fun to look them over, and also see how the new P15's are being built. As you place your order, you'll be able to discuss it with someone who can answer your questions, and show you examples of what you might want. Of course, this has many advantages over using a phone, or computer. Just Remember to stay within your framework as you place your order.

You can always add on later, which is much easier than removing options you've paid for and find you don't need.

When shopping for a used boat, select high, medium, and low priced boats when looking at used Potters. This will give you a general sense of what the market has to offer. However, use caution, price doesn't always indicate the boats condition. There are some exceptions out there, and some of those could be bargains, while others may need unseen expensive repairs.

So, how can you tell the difference? First, gain as much market experience as you can. As you compare Potters, the over priced boats will soon reveal themselves, while those in poor condition will stand apart from the others. Generally speaking, the best boats will be positioned in the middle to the upper part of the market.

When looking at boats, always check the sails, motor, and trailer. Each one of those items will cost about a thousand dollars each to replace new. They're a big part of the price you're being asked to pay for the boat. Climb into the boat and check the bilge for water, which could indicate leaking. See that the boat is properly supported on it's trailer. Ask about it's history, and if there's anything that's not working, or needs repair.

As you continue your search for a Potter, the process of elimination will guide you toward the boat you want. Once you've found your boat, and come to an agreement on price, it never hurts to ask for a demonstration sail. You'll learn a lot about the boat, and get to sail it too. After the sail, payment and ownership papers are exchanged. Now you've become a new Potter skipper, congratulations!

2

Getting it in the Water

Trailering

A trailer is an important part of your Potter's equipment and provides you with the option of choosing many interesting places to sail.

Understanding this makes it easier to justify maintaining your trailer. Most P15 skippers know this, and have told me that almost forty percent of their maintenance is done on the trailer. This is especially true if you sail in salt water. Salt compounds trailer problems. It breaks down the grease used to lubricate wheel bearings and shorts out the trailer lights. Nuts and bolts become frozen, making repairs difficult. Meanwhile, rust develops everywhere as the trailer ages even when it's washed down with fresh water.

How long has it been since your trailer was last serviced? If your answer is "I don't know," you need to reconsider that, to avoid being stranded somewhere along the highway.

Routine inspections of your trailer are a good idea. Trailer lights need to be tested before going out on the road. Tires and wheel bearings should be inspected for wear or damage. Check for under inflated tires which lower your gas mileage and wear out more quickly. Take a look at the trailer springs, because after repeated immersion over the years, they can rust to the point of failure. Of course, all this seems like a lot to do, but once your trailer is in good condition, it only has to be dealt with periodically.

Almost any small car can pull a P15. However, it's wise to check your vehicle operators manual. Not only do you need the power to pull, but the breaks to stop. Ask yourself, is your trailer adjusted to fit your boat and car? A P15 and its trailer weigh about six hundred pounds. This means that about ten percent of that weight should be placed on the car's ball hitch.

It's easy to check the tongue weight if you have a bathroom scale. Most trailers have a wheel jack. Using a stepping stool, crank the tongue of the trailer up and place it on the stool. Then after cranking the wheel up, slip a bathroom scale under it. Let the wheel down onto the scale to find the tongue weight. Sometimes the tongue weight on the ball is too much, and adjustments must be made.

If your trailer's axel is adjustable, you can slide it forward. If not, then you must move the Potter back on it's trailer. When I first got my P15, the trailer tongue weight was one hundred seventy pounds. To correct this, I moved the axle forward.

I marked the axle's original position with a pencil on the trailer frame to check my progress. Then I slacked the bolts that secure the axle to the trailer. Using a rope, a bridle was made and secured to the axle near each wheel. Taking the retrieval strap from the winch, I ran it down under the trailer and secured it to the bridle, then took up the slack. As tension was put on the strap, the axle would move forward, then bind, first on one side and then the other. Leaving the tension on the strap, I would rap on the axle near each wheel with a rubber mallet, eventually shifting it to the full forward position. Using the original pencil marks, I checked to see that the axle was square to the trailer before bolting it down.

Finding the tongue weight still too heavy, meant that the Potter had to be slid back on its trailer. I found the easiest way to do that was to launch the Potter and move the trailer's bow stanchion back. Because of the limited space allowed for the boat's storage, a measurement was taken of the overall length of the boat and trailer to see if it would fit in its storage space. I also found it important to consider how the tie down strap would be affected once the Potter was moved back on its trailer.

To avoid damage to the hull, a P15 must be given good support while on it's trailer. You'll need support along each side of the hull and the keel where the centerboard is. This is done with long rectangular boards called bunks which are carpeted to protect the hull. Many Potter trailers have several rollers for additional hull support and protection. One is under the bow, and the other serves as a fender on the bow stanchion. A tie down strap is used to secure the bow of the boat to the stanchion and an additional strap is led across the cockpit to prevent the boat from shifting on the bunks when traveling.

Many Potter trailers have guides. These are vertical poles attached to the sides of the trailer. Often, they're covered with plastic pipe which serve as rollers to help protect the boat as it's pulled onto the trailer. Guides are very helpful when retrieving the boat in a crosswind situation. They also make it easy to see the empty trailer when backing it down the ramp. Most P15 trailers have this equipment. If you mark the plastic rollers with tape they'll tell you when the water is deep enough to launch the boat.

I remember taking delivery of my Potter at the factory in Los Angles. We entered the freeway during the last of the morning rush hour in heavy rain. I had not pulled a trailer in years, and was very nervous about it, however, all went well. It just takes time, and a little practice to get used to it.

Here are some trailering points you may want to consider. When making turns, the trailer wheel will cut inside the turn your vehicle makes, so watch the trailer with the side mirror to avoid hitting curbs or other objects. This is especially true with tight turns. Keep more distance between yourself and the car ahead to allow for predictable stops. After all, you don't want to change your P15 into a P12 just because you were following too close and then were rear ended. Trailer lights can be a big problem when they don't work well. It's best to replace them with something better. This saves money and trouble in the long run, making trailering much easier.

When towing in traffic, you may hear a bang when starting or stopping. If that happens, pullover somewhere safe and check the trailer hitch. Sometimes the tongue doesn't drop down over the ball. When you hitch up the trailer, check to see that the tongue has dropped down and is properly connected. For added safety, cross your trailer's connecting chains. This should keep the tongue from hitting the pavement if it comes off the ball. Should that happen, coast to the side of the road rolling to a stop to avoid the trailer from ramming your vehicle.

Always be prepared to change a flat tire when towing your Potter. If you're not sure what that requires, try using your car jack to put on the spare trailer tire at home. Take your time, and learn as you go. Removing the rusted lug nuts is the biggest challenge. Part of your trailer maintenance will be to make sure you're up to that task. Oil helps. Should disaster strike, this kind of preparation will pay off, turning a possible crisis into a familiar exercise.

Rigging

If you're the new owner of a Potter, you'll need take time to sort out the rigging. This is best done in your driveway, or the storage yard where you keep your boat.

When I first rigged the Potter, my crew and I worked hard at it, taking more than an hour. Even with practice, it still took forty-five minutes. It wasn't until I began watching other Potter sailors that I was able to cut another fifteen minutes from my rigging time. That savings in time was the result of modifying the rigging, and learning the sequence of steps necessary. Much of the waisted time had been spent going back to get forgotten items and climbing in and out of the boat.

International Marine, the manufacturer, puts out a "Users Guide" for new P15 owners. Even if you've purchased a used boat, ask them to send you the guide. They can be reached on line. The guide will cover P15 rigging in great detail. If you need new parts or sails the manufacturer will also be glad to help. Whenever you buy something from International Marine you're supporting them, just as they continue to support us.

To make rigging your Potter quick and easy, organization is necessary. Some Potter owners, who are new to sailing, become discouraged when attempting to rig, launch, or retrieve their boats. It seems like too much work for too little pleasure, and soon becomes overwhelming. The end result often leads to seldom sailing and then selling the boat after the first year or so. This can be easily avoided when you develop an efficient procedure for rigging your boat. Some of this procedure has to do with how well your boat is set up, but the rest of it depends on how efficiently you work. Working efficiently is not hard, you just have to think about what you're doing and what comes next.

One of the best ways to learn about rigging is to watch other Potter skippers when they arrive at the ramp. Most of the experienced skippers leave a lot of their Potter rigging set up.

Let's take a look. Even with the mast down, the side stays, or shrouds as they are known, remain fastened and ready for sailing. The slack part of the stays are brought forward along the mast and secured with bungee cords. Also,the jib halyard is attached to the jib tack fitting at the bow, and is ready to support the mast once it's raised. The jib sheets are left rigged, and can easily be attached to the jib with a toggle. Looking inside the boat, we see that halyards and sheets have been led through the hatchway during trailering. In the cabin, the mainsail is furled on it's boom, with the mainsheet and traveler still attached. Snaps and shackles are used everywhere possible, to cut down on the time it would take to tie knots.

However, this is only half the story when it comes to rigging. The skipper's movement about the boat must be very efficient to save time and effort.

For example, as the skipper gets out of the car, he opens its rear hatch. Then taking the motor out, locks it in place on the stern of the boat. Walking quickly around the boat, he releases all the sheets, halyards, and tie-downs . He stows the hatch board after opening the hatch. Then climbing aboard, the mast is raised, and held in position with the jib halyard. Now, the boom is brought out and connected to the topping lift, which will support it's aft end as the skipper attaches the gooseneck to the mast. After snapping the traveler in place, the mainsail is bent on using a special gate, allowing you to download the sail slugs into the mast slot. The boom vang is brought up from the cabin and snapped into place along with the main downhaul. Everything else that's needed in the cabin is shifted into the cockpit.

After getting off the boat, the skipper finishes rigging while standing alongside. The rudder, and tiller are attached, and the rudder blade is lifted to keep it from being damaged while launching. All the docking lines and fenders are rigged and ready. Moving forward, the skipper attaches the jib stay, bends on the jib and it's downhaul, then connects the jib sheets and halyard. The rear mast support and tie-down strap are put in the car. As the skipper steps back to inspect his work, we notice it took him a little under thirty minutes to rig his boat.

The skippers order of progression throughout the task leaves little wasted time or effort. While on the boat, he restricted his activity to the cockpit, avoiding the deck, and a possible fall. He didn't waste time climbing in and out of the boat or going back and forth for forgotten items. Although it's not visible to us, the equipment in the cabin is organized into two groups, one on each side of the centerboard trunk, to protect the smaller pieces of equipment from damage by the larger ones. Stacked equipment is organized so the next thing needed will be on top. This is easy to do, because putting the equipment away is done in the reverse order of taking it out. As the skipper rigged the boat, some tasks were left unfinished until he was down alongside the boat. This saves time, and makes the work easier. A good example of this type of planning was leaving the mast standing with the jib halyard until it was time to bend on the jib. Also, the rudder was left in the cockpit. The skipper put it on only after he was working alongside the boat, which is much easier. The whole idea here is to work smart, not hard. Once you find a procedure for rigging your boat that works, commit it to memory and use it each time. Using efficient procedures throughout make rigging and sailing so much easier.

Unrigging your Potter is done in the reverse order. However, there are some steps where tips may be helpful. When stowing your motor and rudder, wash the salt off first using a hand pump garden sprayer. It will save time from having to unload the motor and rudder for washing once you're home. It also keeps the salt out of the boat. The sprayer can come in handy when you get back from sailing, and find gulls and pigeons have made a home out of the top of your car. Extra towels are helpful too. Once you've removed the jib, put it in the back of your car. It's much easier to fold at home. Securing the jib halyard to the jib tack fitting at the bow with maximum tension will make it easier to release the jib stay. Also, if you have trouble inserting or removing the mast pin, (this is with the newer boats) slack the jib halyard, so you'll have enough play to slip the pin in or out.

When leaving, always give the boat a walk around inspection before trailering.

Remember, rigging a Potter is not that difficult. Just be patient, it will become easier and faster, as you gain experience and develop a process that works. The more you use your boat, the easier and faster it will be to rig.

Launching

Launching has a lot in common with rigging, because of it's step by step progression. What makes it different, is having to adjust your activities to cooperate with others using the ramp. If you haven't had a trailer boat before, or little experience with launching boats, sometimes unforeseen problems come up. For now, let's watch a Potter skipper as he moves through a successful launching, just to get the idea.

After arriving in the launching area, the skipper first looks over his surroundings. He hasn't been here before. He checks for any overhanging trees or power lines in the launching area and on the way to the ramp. Taking just a moment to watch others, he learns how launching is done at this ramp.

Once his boat is rigged, everything is stowed. Putting on his flotation vest, he gets into his car, lowers the window and turns off the radio. This helps increase awareness of his surroundings. Backing down the ramp, he stops when the wheels of the trailer touch the water. Making sure that the car is safely parked on the ramp, he disconnects the safety chain and strap at the bow of the boat. He then continues backing down the ramp, stopping when the water touches the mark on the trailer guide showing it's deep enough to launch. Leaving the car safely secured again, he walks out on the float. The boat is pulled off the trailer with its stern line. As it drifts alongside the float, the line is thrown into the cockpit. Grabbing the bow pulpit, the skipper turns the Potter away from the ramp, and guides it to the end of the float using both the bow and stern lines. This signals to anyone using the ramp that the Potter is an outbound boat and the ramp is not being used. As soon as the boat is secured, the car and trailer are removed, parked and locked.

After returning to his Potter, and stepping aboard lightly, he lowers the centerboard and rudder. The motor is started and allowed to warm up. After a few minutes, the lines are cast off, and the skipper motors out onto the bay.

Earlier, I mentioned problems not easily foreseen. These include accidents that happen at boat ramps. Many of these are caused from being stressed out as people wait on you to finish using the ramp. You find yourself beginning to rush, becoming unfocused and open to the possibility of an accident. An accident at the boat ramp won't save anyone time. To guard against this, possibility, always remain calm and watchful, seeing to your safety and that of the boat first.

Always check your route from the rigging area to the ramp. Driving into over hanging trees is a sure way to bring your mast down. If you keep your window open and radio off while driving slowly you'll hear it coming as the mast begins to break through small branches, or just maybe, somebody will yell before you drive under a overhanging obstruction. Many launching facilities serve mostly power boats, and are not very concerned about mast clearance. Right or wrong, they leave that to you.

Steep boat ramps also have their special dangers. For example, after failing to position the boat on the ramp correctly, a second successful attempt is made. Just as the skipper is about to launch his Potter, he notices that it had slid back about two feet on its trailer. At the time, he doesn't believe this is possible, but it probably happened when he accelerated back up the ramp to reposition the trailer. The lesson is clear, from that day on, his boat is never disconnected from the trailer until it's correctly positioned on the ramp and ready for launching.

As I was rigging my boat at a Potter event there was a loud boom. Everyone stopped what they were doing and went to the ramp. It was a sad scene. There on the concrete ramp, three feet from the water sat a Potter. Of course, in sympathy, we all helped get the boat back in the water. With several of us lifting, fenders were placed under the keel and the Potter was rolled into the water. Always use extra caution when driving or walking on a boat ramp at low tide. They can be very slippery. When leaving your car on the ramp, always make sure it's secure. Occasionally, cars are known to launch themselves.

Retrieving

As we watch, a returning Potter skipper motors in and ties his boat close to the ramp. Once back at his car, he puts on his rubber boots before backing the trailer down the ramp. Untying his boat, he leads it onto the trailer. This is done by pulling the Potter forward with it's stern line, and using the bow line as a guide. Now, stepping cautiously down on the ramp, the skipper wades through the water and climbs up on the trailer next to the winch. Because the trailer is below the surface, with the water at the launching marks, the Potter is already more than halfway on the trailer. The skipper has found it saves time to grab the bow pulpit and pull the Potter up on the trailer as far as possible before connecting retrieval strap. The boat is winched in until the bow is secured firmly against the roller, then the safety chain is connected.

In the parking lot, the skipper checks to see if the boat is centered on it's trailer, but finds the Potter's rail against the trailer guide. Giving the Potter a hard shove from the side will center the boat, but If you're unable to do that, in my experience, the Potter will center itself when trailering. The motor and rudder are given a quick wash down, and dried with a towel before being removed. The rudder is stowed in the cockpit. After checking that both the fuel and breather are shut off, the motor is removed and placed in the car. Both the tie down strap and the mast support, are taken from the car and put in the boat. Next, the docking lines and fenders are placed on the bridge deck ready for stowing. Now the skipper moves forward and removes the jib, leaving the jib sheets on deck. As he returns from putting the jib in the car, the jib halyard is connected to the jib tack fitting at the bow. Moving to the cockpit, he tensions the jib halyard, putting slack in the jib stay, making it easy to remove. The jib sheets are looped over the bow cleat, and their slack is taken in. The mast support is put in place.

Now it's time to get into the boat. Everything in the cockpit is stowed below in the order needed for rigging. Next the mainsail is removed from the mast. The boom with the sail furled on it is stowed below. Putting the aft end of the boom in first makes it easier to stow because the sail is less bulky. With the contemporary P15 method the mast is allowed to rotate down into its support, which is fastened to the rudder gudgeons on the transom. If you have an older boat, the mast is first lifted, then slid forward on your shoulder to the balance point as it comes down. Before getting out of the boat, the skipper brings up the bungee cords, hatch slide, and lock from down below.

Once out of the boat, the skipper secures the mast. The halyards are brought forward and guided around the mast cleats near the base of the mast then pulled aft to be secured. Both the shrouds and jib stay are also secured forward along the mast using the bungee cords. After all the excess lines are put in the cabin, the hatch board is slid into place and locked. Just the tie down strap is left to do. With that done, everything is complete. Finally the boat is inspected to see that all is secure before going back on the road.

Now that you've seen how other Potters rig and launch as they come and go, this will make it easier to quickly get your own boat in the water for sailing. Be patient, it does take some time and effort before you're able to make all this look easy, but it's worth it, and while alone or with other Potters you'll be rewarded with many good sailing memories.

3

The Daily Cruise

Potters do more day sailing than any other activity, and once underway just sail for pleasure. Often, Potters are found sailing along attractive shorelines in shallow areas, or in a quiet cove for a picnic lunch. All this is done in a kicked back sort of way. This relax and enjoy attitude is at the very heart of pottering. However, just below the surface of that attitude is one of quiet awareness.

Such awareness requires observation, planning ahead, and good decision making. These are the tools that skippers use to keep themselves and their crews safe while out on the water. Skippers know that both wind and water conditions change, sometimes for the better, and sometimes not.

In this chapter, if you're new to P15s or to sailing, you'll learn how to take the anxiety out of using your Potter. Always remember, that anytime something is new, tension always exists.

The first time I sailed my schooner, I kept thinking, twenty-four thousand pounds of boat, and over six-hundred square feet of sail. As time went by, necessity made it a familiar drill just to sail her back into the berth because once again the engine had failed.

Preparation

Before going sailing for the first time, you'll want to prepare for it. All the safety equipment required by the Coast Guard and the state you live in need to be aboard your boat. As skipper, it'll be your responsibility to know how and when to use it. If you have limited experience, taking a volunteer Coast Guard Auxiliary class will bring you up to speed on many boating subjects.

A fire on board your Potter is a big safety issue, especially if you're on the water. I say this, because over the years, I've fought two on the water and one on shore. With this in mind, it's very important to know where to locate your fire extinguishers. A good location for a fire extinguisher is on the divider that separates the under cockpit area from the two stowage bins at the head of the bunks. This way, they're in reach through the hatches from the cockpit or from down below in the cabin. Two fire extinguishers are not overkill. In fact, one extinguisher failed to put out the last fire I experienced. It was started when the Potter's shrouds, which were stowed down below at the time, came into contact with both battery terminals while trailering. The other more obvious source of fire, would be the fuel you carry for your stove or motor. These must be safely stored in a vented area away from any source of flame.

When sailing, you'll need charts of the area you intend to navigate. Keep your charts at hand and become familiar with them. From the deck of a

Potter, much of your navigation is visual, but using your chart as you sail will provide other needed information such as depth of water, buoy identification, good holding ground for anchoring, and coves to anchor in.

In open water, when aids to navigation or landmarks are not visible, a GPS is needed. Plot important waypoints on your chart. Your first waypoint should be plotted at the harbor entrance, then you can plot waypoints out from there. As they're plotted on your chart, label them the same way you have them in your GPS. Navigate with these waypoints during good weather to gain confidence before you're challenged by darkness or fog.

If you're sailing in salt water, you'll also need a tide book. This will tell you the direction and velocity of currents, as well as the times for highs, lows, and the slack water of each tide. When planning a day sail, it's best to take advantage of tidal currents.

Always check the weather before going sailing. Only choose weather and wind velocities that are fun to sail in. Potters can be sailed in more than thirty knots of wind.

While realizing this, it's not really something you'll want to do. It's very hard on equipment and quite difficult physically. Five to ten knots is much more fun, and that's what sailing's all about.

A hand held VHF radio can be a very useful tool when sailing. It can be used to contact friends for rendezvous or a harbor master for making reservations at the marina. The VHF is a good source of weather information and is monitored by the Coast Guard. There are rules for using a VHF that should be learned. If you decide to get one, read the instructions carefully.

Docking

After launching, you'll need good docking lines for tying up your Potter. They make it easier to secure your boat, especially when it's windy. Using three eighths inch nylon, in twenty foot lengths will do the job. That may seem unusually long; however, picture this, a cross wind is blowing at about ten knots, pushing your Potter sideways away from the float. Using twenty foot lines makes docking in these conditions much easier. You step off the boat with both bow and stern lines in your hand. Quickly you loop the stern line under the horn of the docking cleat nearest the stern of your boat. As you walk forward carrying your stern line, the bow line is cleated. Having the stern line still in your hand allows you to control the boat as you return to secure it. Now, try this with ten foot lines. It doesn't quite work. Docking lines should always be longer than the overall length of a small boat.

Rules of the Road

Knowing the nautical rules of the road will go a long way toward taking the worry out of sailing your Potter. As larger faster boats bear down on you, knowing who has the right of way does offer some comfort.

However, the skipper coming at you may have no idea what the rules are, or may not see you. So It's best to stay on the defensive, and take evasive action when you sense a possible conflict. You can do this by taking a bearing on the other boat before it gets close. Place some part of your boat, for instance a shroud or jib stay, between your eye and the other vessel to serve as a range for a bearing. If the bearing is changing the other vessel will pass by. If it isn't, the other vessel is either moving directly toward or away from you. Read the hull language of the on-coming boat to help determine its direction. Is the other boat's course predictable? Where will it be when your courses cross? If you feel the other boat's too close, change your course now and stick to it until the other boat has passed. The sooner you do this the safer you'll be. As you're sailing, always keep a watch, not just ahead, but all around.

Commit these following rules to memory. They'll keep you out of trouble in most situations.

When motoring, your Potter is a powerboat, even with the sails up. As a powerboat, you must give way to: all vessels towing, hand powered craft, sailboats, and all commercial vessels. Other powerboats crossing your course from the right side will expect you to give way. Powerboats approaching head to head should move to their right, but are not required to. Overtaking boats do not have the right of way.

As a sailboat your Potter should give way to: all vessels towing, hand powered craft, and all commercial vessels. When sailboats are on opposite tacks, starboard tack (wind on the right side) has the right of way. When sailboats are on the same tack, the leeward (downwind) boat has the right of way. Sailboats do not have the right of way when overtaking any other boat. If you are being overtaken by another boat, you are obligated to hold your course until the other boat has passed and is clear ahead.

The rules that I've given here are not technically complete, but they're enough to get you through most situations until you can find a book on the rules. For that, I highly recommend the "One Minute Guide to the Nautical Rules of the Road" by Charlie Wing. It's published by McGraw-Hill and is an excellent reference. I keep a copy in my Potter for uncommon situations.

Being on the water is different because you can't just walk away when things becomes difficult. For that reason, an independent spirit is required. Once out on the water, you must make your own decisions. Hopefully, you'll have other Potter skippers to mentor you along the way. Learn as much as you can from them, but always make your own decisions based on sound information. If you make a mistake, and we all do, you'll quickly learn from it. This is how you gain experience.

Good skippers always observe, taking the time to collect information before making a decision. They focus first on what's most important, and do one task at a time. If I had to condense fifty years of sailing experience, this paragraph would probably be it.

Beginning Anchoring

Anchoring is a fairly broad subject and you need to read up on it. There's nothing particularly difficult about it, but you should be familiar with it. The basics are certainly worth covering here. Anchoring can be done under power or sail. If your experience is limited, using power is easier, but don't let the anchor line foul your propeller. As a small boat sailor, you may have little experience with anchoring. If this is the case, start by anchoring out for lunch. This way, you can remain in the cockpit watching to see that your anchor doesn't drag. Dragging, as you probably know, is what happens when the anchor isn't holding. There are several reasons for this. Either the anchor isn't designed for the bottom it's trying to grip or it was set poorly.

Most Potters use a "Fortress" type anchor with triangular flukes that stow flat and hold well in mud and sand. Attached to the anchor with a shackle is fifteen feet of quarter inch chain, and a hundred feet of three eighths inch line.

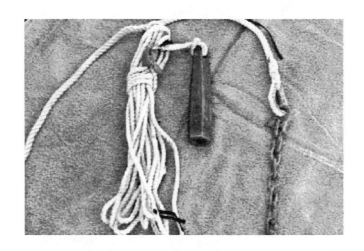

The line has an eye splice around a steel thimble
and is shackled to the chain. All the shackle pins
must be wired so they don't work loose. Both the
chain and line are marked in fathoms, at six foot
intervals, with short pieces of parachute cord or
rawhide. These are woven through the strands of the
line or tied to the chain to serve as markers showing
how much line you've let out. Along with that you'll
also need a lead line marked in fathoms. The lead
line can have a one pound fishing weight attached to
one end of the line, or the traditional lead used on
larger boats. Your lead line only needs to be about
five fathoms long, or thirty feet, unless you anchor in
very deep water. All of this equipment is collectively

called ground tackle, and should be stowed together where it can be reached quickly. Ground tackle is an important part of your Potter's safety gear. Once you've selected your anchorage, check your chart to see if the bottom has good holding ground for the anchor you're using, and note how deep the water is. Use the lead line to confirm the actual depth due to tide. Figure out how much line you'll need to let out. Bring your boat to a stop then slowly back away as you lower the anchor. While it bumps along the bottom, you'll begin to feel the anchor grab as you hold the line in your hands. Once the line becomes taut you can set it by using just a little power from the motor. Then let out some extra scope, just to be safe.

Scope is the ratio of line let out to the depth of water. Most anchor manufacturers recommend using a scope of seven times the depth of water for the best holding power. This may not be possible if the anchorage is crowded, or necessary if there's hardly any wind while you're there. You be the judge. If the wind does come up just let out more scope.

Some Potter skippers anchor from the cockpit. This makes sense because being in the cockpit is where the controls for the boat are. Once anchored, you can lead the anchor line forward and cleat it off at the bow. Then your Potter will turn to face the wind. Just remember, the key to successful anchoring is practice.

Motoring

Many Potters use two-horsepower Honda outboard motors. They're reliable and preform well. For this reason, they'll be the focus of our discussion here.

If you're new to sailing, or have just bought a Potter, motoring is a good place to start. Motoring doesn't require as many skills as sailing and it's easier to learn. Gaining confidence when motoring will give you something to fall back on when sailing becomes too challenging especially in the early stages of learning. If you already sail, learning how to handle your Potter under power is still important. Too often, motoring is just brushed off as a quick way to get in and out of the harbor. This, I think, comes from the attitude that motors are bad and sails are good.

Even though no one mentions it, Potters are really auxiliary sloops. Because of this, you can motor while sailing, or any other time you want. This advantage gives you more flexibility on the water. It increases the distance you can travel in a day, while allowing you access into places too narrow or shallow for sailing. This is just one more example of how using your Potter to its full potential increases its value.

The procedure for starting a Honda outboard is simple. It's best remembered as five basic steps. If you forget a step, the motor either won't start, or if it does, won't run for very long. Count the steps off as you go.

Because we have to start somewhere, the beginning step will be to open the breather on the fuel cap. Next, on the left side of the motor, slide the fuel shutoff lever aft to open it. Pull the choke out. It's the black button on the left. Then open the throttle to the start position. The last step is to pull the starter cord, while using your other hand to hold the motor down. When it starts, it will run roughly until the choke is pushed in. As you do this, use your other hand to throttle down the motor and prevent the boat from charging ahead. To stop the motor, push in the red button on the lower right.

When sailing your Potter, you'll want to lift the motor up out of the water for better performance. First, close the breather on the fuel cap and shut off the fuel by moving the lever forward. If this isn't done before lifting the motor, it will flood and fail to start when needed. It can be restarted after its been flooded if you put the motor back down in the water and let it sit so the excess fuel can drain before restarting.

When gas gets old, it loses its octane power. Because of this, your motor may not start. This is solved by adding stabilizer to your gas, or rotating the older gas left in the fuel container into your car every three or four weeks.

Never turn your motor upside down. Because the Honda is a four cycle motor, oil will drain into the cylinder head making it impossible to start.

After an hour or so of motoring in your Potter, you'll probably begin to wonder when it's going to run out of gas. There are three different ways to answer this. Learning from experience, you'll discover that if you run your motor in the start position it will go for about an hour and forty-five minutes before it needs refueling. If you forget, it will tell you when it needs gas, by sounding different about ten seconds before it stops. Another way to answer the fuel question is to make a dipstick for your tank.

The dipstick method is more accurate, but does have a downside. To check your fuel level you must throttle back to idle, to limit vibration for an accurate reading on the dip stick.

Making a dipstick for a Honda is easy. Here are the measurements taken from the bottom of the stick which is seven and a quarter inches long. The first mark is at one half inch. That's the out of gas mark. The second mark is one and a quarter inch, the third mark is two inches, the fourth mark is two and three quarter inches, and the fifth mark is three and five eights inches. The last measurement marks one full liter of fuel. Use a saw to cut all the marks on the dipstick. The tank will hold more, but the stick is not marked for that.

When fueling, try to find a place in calm water away from traffic. Get the fuel container ready to pour. Remove the fuel cap from the motor and place it in the cockpit to avoid losing it. The fuel cap connection can be pulled out of the tank accidentally by the nozzle of the fuel container. The penalty for losing the fuel cap is about thirty dollars. After fuelir

any spill with a cloth before restarting the mo.

Sometimes just quietly motoring along sight seeing

can be very enjoyable. It adds variety to your

Pottering, and also expands your horizons.

Boat Handling Under Power

Handling your Potter under power will only take a

short time to master. Once you understand the

basics, then it's just a matter of going out and doing

it.

When motoring long distances, you'll need to trim

your Potter to get the best out of it. Let go of the tiller

to see if the boat tracks straight. If not, turn the

outboard motor until it does. If you're motoring, lift

the centerboard about three quarters of the way up.

You don't need it's drag in the water. Start a slow

turn, if the boat doesn't respond, lower the

centerboard just enough until it does. Don't forget to

lower the centerboard before making tight turns or

sailing. Move forward in the cockpit. Lifting the stern

ecreases drag. Set your throttle for start when cruising under power. It will give good economy and move the boat close to hull speed.

Wakes or waves must be managed when powering. The worst of these come from large boats that don't slow down. These waves can be three feet or higher and breaking. As the waves move toward you, check for traffic before turning into them. Slow down as they approach, but not to the point of losing steering control. Once you're over the first three or four you can usually return safely to your course.

As tidal currents run against the wind, waves will become steeper and more apt to break. Keep your speed up when powering into waves, but avoid putting your bow through them, because they'll stop the boat. A balance must be maintained between excessive speed and steering control as the following example demonstrates.

Years ago, I was the helmsman on a twenty-six foot steam launch called Fearless. After spending time anchored in a sheltered cove for lunch, we decided to return to the yacht harbor. As we entered the bay from our cove, the ebb tide quickly swept us away leaving little chance of return. The wind, since our time in the cove, had more than doubled, blowing hard against an ebb tide.

The launch was like most of her type, and designed with a fine clipper bow, narrow beam, and an upright iron boiler. She was never meant to be in the conditions we were in now.

Several sailboats were swept by in the high winds, one with a broken mast at the spreaders, and another with a blown out mainsail. A sudden gust pushed our bow away from the waves just as one broke onto the foredeck knocking the launch down. The cockpit combing was driven well underwater leaving the floor boards floating. Yelling back to the engineer, I asked for more power, and Fearless, somewhat reluctantly, came back up to face the waves again. Because of this situation, we could not turn around. To do so meant certain capsize. Our only way to safety was to allow the ebb tide to push us up to a windward shore that would provide shelter.

After several more waves over the bow, the launch was slowed until her bow just barely cleared each crest by inches, but with enough speed that steering control was maintained. I continued to hold her head to the wind, with little or no progress through the waves. After what seemed like forever, it was the ebb current that finally took us to safety.

Well, there you are, powering along with your Potter all trimmed out, thinking everything is just fine when your hat blows off. Quickly, the centerboard is lowered, the motor is slowed and the tiller is pushed over. As the Potter completes it's circle, the hat sweeps by and you pluck it from the water. "It's a good thing I happen to be sitting on the same side as the motor," you think. " I should just sit here all the time when motoring. All I have to do is turn the boat so the object I want comes right alongside."

If it were a person in the water instead of a hat, you would have to pick them up on the other side of the boat, away from the motor and closest to the boarding ladder. As you approach the person in the water, have them face you to fend off the boat. Lead them to the boarding ladder. Lower the ladder to help them aboard. If they're too cold to come up the ladder, then you'll have to pull them into the boat. Failing that, grab the mainsheet, and tie them to the boat until you can get help. Getting them out of cold water quickly is important to their survival.

While we're in the process of picking up hats and people, let's learn about motoring in tight spaces. This is easy to learn and will build your confidence with a little practice in open water.

Several years ago at the Cruiser Challenge in Monterey, I took a wrong turn in the harbor motoring into a narrow dead end looking for my assigned berth. It wasn't wide enough to turn around using my rudder. For this reason several people stopped what they were doing to watch.

With the outboard in slow forward, I put the shock cord on the tiller to hold it straight. The motor was rotated a hundred and eighty degrees, which is reverse. Without touching the throttle, slowly the Potter came to a stop, but just before it began to back up I turned the motor ninety degrees to the right. The

Potter responded by rotating in its own length one hundred and eighty degrees from it's original course. After returning the motor to its forward position the boat powered out of the dead end.

A lee shore is anything that the wind is going to blow your Potter onto if the motor stops. So, it's always a good idea to have your halyards hooked up to your sails before leaving the dock under power. Even as reliable as they are, motors sometimes stop without warning. Being prepared with your sails as a back up makes sense.

Perhaps it was one of those plastic grocery store bags that fouled your propeller, or maybe you forgot to open the air vent on the motor. Whatever it was doesn't matter at this moment because you're going on the rocks. There are several things you can do to avoid this. The first is planning. Always give yourself plenty of sea room. Any course you choose along a lee shore should allow for enough time to anchor, or get some sail up when the motor stops.

Towing

If your outboard isn't working and there's no wind, you might want to consider a tow if it's offered. This just might get you home on time, which is good news. The bad news is that you are dependent upon the skills of the skipper doing the towing. If he's good, he'll keep his speed down to less than your maximum hull speed, and a member of his crew will watch your boat ready to relay any message.

However, just the opposite could happen. For example, your towing skipper quickly accelerates to ten knots and beyond, making water shoot out of your centerboard trunk like a whale spouting. You're yelling for the towing skipper to stop, but he can't hear you over the roar of this twin engines. His motto is never look back. Attempting to stop the flooding, you stuff a sail bag into the centerboard slot, soaking yourself in the process. There you sit, white knuckled with both hands on the tiller and a bow wave almost as high as the the cabin top wondering what happens next, sinking, or arriving at the boat ramp. The worst could be yet to come. Maybe he'll take you right into the marina and cast you off a few boat lengths from the ramp at five knots. I know this is overly exaggerated, but I've seen some of these things happen. You'll probably have a better experience next time if you use a canoe paddle, or take a tow from a slower boat.

If you're the one doing the towing, there are several things you'll need to know. Towing is a team effort. Both skippers involved in towing need to keep an open line of communication. The lead skipper needs to be watchful of the boat being towed. The skipper being towed needs to follow in the tow boat's wake. When a towline is attached to the stern cleat of the towboat, it's ability to maneuver is restricted. If this happens, the towboat needs to throttle back, putting some slack in the line to regain steering control before trying a difficult turn. When entering the harbor with a tow, be careful. At some point, the towline will need to be cast off leaving the towed boat with just enough momentum to reach the dock safely.

Make sure the towline isn't just dropped in the water and allowed to foul the propeller.

Boat Handling Under Sail

Handling your Potter under sail is more complicated than using power. You're not pushing buttons or pulling levers to get results. Sailing takes understanding the forces of both wind and water, and how they'll affect your boat. As we cover this, it's assumed that you have a basic knowledge of sailing and it's vocabulary. If this is not the case there is a glossary in the back of the book which will be of some help.

If you're new to sailing, and have just purchased your Potter, you'll probably want to get it in the water as soon as possible. However, be careful about doing this, because your first sailing experiences need to be good ones. Pick a day with winds of five knots for your first sail. It's best to sail upwind first as this will make returning to the ramp easier later in the day.

The wind will often build in the afternoon. If this makes you anxious, then it's time to stop sailing. As a beginner, the dream you have of sailing is a fragile one, and can easily be broken with a series of bad experiences. Don't talk yourself into continuing to sail just because others are. Be your own skipper. If the wind is beyond your comfort level get the sails down and start motoring. If you still want to be out on the water, you can always motor up wind, then sail back down to the ramp with only the jib up as you watch others sail. As a new sailor you'll want to build positive experiences that you can bank on. Because of this, it's important to choose only the best conditions which will certainly expand as you gain more experience. Your goal at the end of the day, should be to feel good about your time on the water, looking forward to more of the same. Even those still out sailing, will not return with a greater reward than that.

As an experienced sailor, you may choose to motor away from the dock with your sails furled just to get clear of other boats, especially when it's crowded.

Getting sail up on the water when you're alone requires extra skills. Experienced skippers know that its best to keep the wind on the starboard side so they don't get hit with the sail when raising it. This will also avoid fouling the topping lift with the sail as it's hauled up. All the mainsail controls including the topping lift should be on the starboard side for best access.

Let's take a minute, and watch one skipper as he raises sail out on the water. After positioning his Potter with the wind blowing over the starboard side, the motor is secured and lifted out of the water. The tiller is kept centered with self steering so the Potter's course will be predictable. The sail ties are quickly taken off and stowed below. After shaking out the furl in the mainsail, he frees the mainsheet and boom vang. As the mainsail begins to go up, it swings to port in the breeze, allowing the skipper to work the main halyard on the starboard side.

As the Potter moves off on a reach, the wind presses the sail against the lee rigging. Rather than fighting the sail, the skipper reaches back and steers his Potter closer to the wind which blows the sail back away from the rigging. After hauling the sail almost to the top, he's stopped by the weight of the boom. He knows that pulling harder will finish the job, but chooses an easier way. Cleating off the halyard, the skipper grabs it again where it comes down along the mast. Using his weight, he pulls the halyard aft raising the mainsail to the top. Holding the halyard in his left hand, he pulls the slack through the cam cleat with his right. Next, he checks the mainsheet to see that it isn't fouled as he pulls it in. Now that he's sailing, the halyard is stowed and the boom vang and downhaul are adjusted. Next, the skipper frees the jib downhaul and jib sheets, checking to see that everything is clear to run before hauling the jib up. Once it's up and sheeted in, the jib downhaul is cleated with some slack in it to allow for future halyard adjustments.

When sailing, experienced skippers always look for signs, just as Indians did in the old west. These signs are clues that can be found in the wind and on the water. For example, when sailing by a buoy you would look for current flowing around it. Estimating the water's speed and direction is useful information you'll need for navigating. Up ahead you'll watch other boats to see how they might be affected by changes in wind strength or direction.

Tide lines, usually seen as ripples on the water and sometimes filled with flotsam, mark conflicting currents, and can slow your progress when sailing on the wrong side of them. Wind patterns that mark the water will show where it's best to sail. There are many signs that can help you on your way and others that will mean trouble. The storm clouds that have moved closer, the fog that's closing in, and the bearings you've taken showing you're being set down on a shoal by the current are all good examples.

A skipper may not speak much of these signs unless you ask about them, but good skippers always watch for them when sailing.

Mainsheet

The mainsheet should be given special care. It should never be sat on or left underfoot. The penalty for such a violation can be a chilling experience that's best avoided as this next example shows.

Many years ago while sailing my friend's twenty-three foot catboat in gusty weather, I was forced to relearn the lesson of the mainsheet. When the gust hit, I was unprepared, and we were knocked down so quickly that I was launched off the windward cockpit seat, finding myself on the mainsail with my legs dangling in the water below the boom. As the catboat spun into the wind, it rudely dumped me back into a cockpit full of cold water. Just as I was getting to my feet, Dave, my Potter crew, who had been standing in the companionway, casually said with a smile, "My, that cockpit sure drains out nicely! "

As a Potter skipper you need to decide how you want to lead your mainsheet. First consider how you use your boat. Do you sail alone or with a crew? Having a crew makes leading the mainsheet from aft on the traveler a good idea. This eliminates having to reach around the crew to trim the sail. The down side is, with the cam cleat riding on the traveler, and not stationary, it doesn't release or cleat as easy as you might want. If you sail alone, a forward location with the cam cleat on the boom is a good option. For a while, my mainsheet was rigged to use from either end, before I finally chose to cleat it up forward on the boom. It's just more accessible from there when single handing, but not as easy to use with a crew.

Back in the seventies, most Potters were rigged to sheet from a fixed cam cleat on the bridge deck. This has lost favor over time, possibly because the cam cleat and sheet were in the way, however, it's still an option to consider.

Another thing to think about is how you're going to keep all that mainsheet out from underfoot, especially when sailing on the wind. If the sheet is rigged forward to a cam cleat on the boom, you can put the mainsheet in the cabin. If you're sheeting from aft, the mainsheet can be left in the rear of the footwell out of the way. The choice is yours, but keep in mind that you must be able to release the mainsheet in two seconds or less from anywhere on the boat during a gust. Practice doing this. It's like the six gun draw in a western movie.

Sometimes the mainsheet can be left in its cam and ignored for hours. At other times, the mainsheet must be held in your hand. Watching for signs of wind on the water will show what to expect.

Movement in the Boat

Now that you've acquired some confidence with your Potter, let's focus on movement in the boat. Any movement you do should be done gently. Banging about in your Potter disrupts the air flow over the sails and water flowing by both the centerboard and rudder.

Any good sailor coming aboard will step lightly, it tells a lot about his experience around boats. Good consistent movement in the boat makes everything better.

Tacking

When tacking efficiently, there are certain moves you make each time you tack. If you're using standard sheeting, it takes a little more work and a longer reach to get the jib in. If you're not fast enough, then it can take two hands when it's breezy.

Here's how tacking is done on a Potter with inside sheeting to the cabin top. The boat is on a port tack with its skipper sitting to windward. The skipper slowly pushes the tiller to lee and the boat begins to luff. The lee jib sheet is released with the left hand. The skipper then moves toward center, pivoting low on one foot while facing forward, shifting his weight to the starboard cockpit bench, as he passes the tiller from his right hand to his left. He then pulls the jib sheet down into the cam on the new tack using his right hand. Sliding his hand up the cleated sheet again he completes trimming the jib. This method can be used while sailing from either the windward or leeward sides.

Jibing

When jibing a Potter, the most important thing to do is anticipate where your weight will be needed. Once the mainsail comes over, you should be facing it. Your weight will help counter the heeling caused by the shock of the mainsail as it fills on the new jibe. There are several ways to shift the boom from one side of the boat to the other when jibing. The most recognized one is sheeting the main in, and then turning the tiller away from the sail until it jibes. As the boom crosses center, the main sheet is left free to run reducing the shock of the jibe. A faster way to do it in light to moderate winds, is to just grab a hand full of main sheet and throw the main over. Because the Potter has such a small mainsail, the forces are not great enough to damage the rigging. During heavy winds, you would want to use caution, carefully sheeting in the sail before jibing it, or avoiding the jibe altogether by heading up and tacking.

If the jib is winged out with the whisker pole, it will need to be jibed. This is one of the more complex maneuvers a single-handed sailor does on a Potter. It must be done quickly and without mistakes. Taking too much time increases the chance that your Potter will round up, or accidentally jibe while you're standing in the companionway.

Once your tiller is set for self-steering, go forward into the companionway, place a foot on the centerboard trunk and use your legs to brace yourself in the companionway while you jibe the pole. First release both jib sheets, then unclip the pole from the mast. Pull the pole in toward you and reattach the jib to the whisker pole for the new jibe to avoid twisting the clew. Jibe the jib over to the other side using the pole and secure it to the mast. Step back into the cockpit and sheet in the jib. If you're using a whisker pole with tangs, then disconnect the pole from the mast and jibe it to the other side by dipping it down to clear the jib stay. To keep the sheet from coming free of the tangs, you must hold the lee sheet in tension, trapped against the pole with your hand. Clip the pole back on the mast, keeping tension on the sheet until the jib is trimmed. Focus on your movement when using the whisker pole, to find the best way for making jibing fast and easy.

Heaving To

One of the most important maneuvers you'll use in sailing is heaving to. Heaving to holds your Potter to the wind so you can take care of your own needs or the boat's while not having to sail. A Potter is hove to by balancing the forces of a back winded jib to windward against the tiller to leeward.

The first time I hove to was in the lee of an island. The wind was quite shifty there. While we had lunch in the cockpit, the wind direction shifted around the compass. No matter which direction the wind came from, even from aft causing a jibe, the boat always returned to the hove to tack. Later when single handing along the coast of Mexico, I would occasionally heave to just to take a time out from the constant motion and noise of sailing to get some sleep. Even in heavier winds, the sloop would bob up over the waves. Her deck would dry off in the sun and all would be quiet down below.

When heaving to, use the same system as when tacking, but don't release the jib. Temporarily, the jib will take control of the boat pushing it away from the wind. Hold the tiller to leeward during this time. The Potter will heel more than usual with a backwinded jib, so you'll need to place yourself on the windward side and be ready to let out the mainsheet if needed until the boat comes almost to a stop. Because the Potter is a centerboard boat, it's best to stay on the windward side when hove to. Secure the tiller to leeward and sheet in the mainsail to keep the boat pointing up if it isn't heeling too much. You're now hove to, barely moving with the wind slightly forward of the beam. Sit for awhile and take a break. Watch how your Potter balances itself. Always keep your mainsheet near by. Because your boat is not moving through the water, she is less stable in gusts, which is normal for all sailboats in this situation. Skippers often heave to for putting on foul weather gear, reefing, and a variety of other reasons. As you look around, maybe you'll see a boat bearing down on you. Getting underway is fast and easy, free the tiller and then the jib. Once the jib is sheeted in you're quickly sailing again. Learning the art of heaving to feels like finding a treasured possession you thought lost forever.

When coming in from sailing after the Cruiser Challenge in Monterey there isn't much sheltered water for getting your sails down. The winds are often about fifteen knots in the afternoon and the water's quite choppy as the large charter boats bring in the fisherman from sea at the end of the day.

In this case, it's best to heave to with the motor to windward, this avoids starting the motor with your weight on the lee side of the boat. Stand in the companionway and use it for support when getting the mainsail down. As you furl the sail, place one foot in the bottom of the cockpit, put your other foot up on the windward bench against the combing while leaning to leeward against the boom for support. This will keep you from losing your balance when using both hands to furl the mainsail. With the mainsail down, your boat will fall away from the wind, but this is not a problem. Next, start your motor. Head downwind and let your jib jibe over to the side it's sheeted on then lower it before heading into the harbor. Using this system allows you to do one thing at a time making it safe and easy to get sail down in rough conditions.

Reefing

When the wind begins to build and your Potter becomes more difficult to control, it's time to reef. Knowing when to reef is important for your safety, and is best done when you first think about it. Reefing reduces heeling, making it easier to steer and sit in the cockpit. Your Potter will go just about as fast when reefed and be more comfortable to sail. When sailing in a group, reefing is a decision that's made by each skipper. Don't depend on an experienced skipper to make that decision for you. Experienced skippers tend to carry more sail longer, reefing quickly at the last moment. Always make your own decisions about reefing. It only takes a moment to let out a reef when the wind goes down.

Reefing can be done three ways. You can reef at the dock where it's more sheltered before sailing. After heaving to on the water, you can reef as you would at the dock. Reefing on the fly is different and done while continuing to sail.

When reefing at the dock, haul your mainsail up to the first reef, and secure the tack of the sail on the hook at the gooseneck near the mast. Tension your main halyard and cleat it. Next the clew reefing line is hauled in, pulling the aft corner of the sail down to the boom. Stand back and look at your mainsail. The foot of the sail between the tack and clew should be flat and the luff taut along the mast. Your reefed sail should not have any more creases in it than normal. If it does, the reefing lines may need to be adjusted. The part of the sail that's hanging below the boom is called the bunt and is left as is, if it's not in your way. If you decide to tie up the bunt, use the small lines called reefing nettles along the foot of the sail. They have stopper knots on each side of the sail keeping them in place. The bunt is tied to the sail, not around the boom. The knot that's used for this is called a reef knot, better known as a square knot. Sailors use this knot because it can be untied with one hand. Just grab one of its ends and yank it back on itself. It will roll over into loose half hitches, which are easily undone with the fingers of one hand. You might want to practice all this in your driveway before you use it out on the water.

After gaining experience reefing at the dock, you'll need to try reefing out on the water. Remember to heave to on the starboard tack before reefing. Then tie in the reef as you did at the dock. When reefing the first couple of times on the water, do it in moderate winds.

There are several tricks that will make reefing easier. Keep a sail stop in your mast slot and lock it in place below the boom before you reef. As you slack the main halyard you won't have to chase the boom as it slides down the mast slot. This makes it much easier to put the tack grommet on the hook. The most difficult part of reefing on the water is pulling the clew down to the boom because the sail still has some wind in it. Releasing the boom vang will help allowing the boom to lift toward reefing clew.

Reefing on the fly is used to avoid being left behind when sailing in a group or racing. It's different from other methods because the boat continues to sail while you reef. To be successful, you must adjust the Potter to sail itself. The jib is left sheeted with a partially luffing main and the tiller secured slightly to lee to help hold course. This helps to counteract the Potter's tendency to fall off the wind when the halyard is slacked for reefing. Watch the boat sail for a moment to see that it's on course before reefing. As you slack the halyard, the boat will begin to fall off away from the wind, so you must work quickly. When finished, free your tiller and sheet in your mainsail to continue sailing.

When putting in a second reef, leave the first one in place. Taking into consideration that the conditions will be difficult, to say the least, it may be best to drop your main leaving the jib up on a starboard tack. Once your main is down, head up wind with your jib sheeted normally. The Potter will sail slowly with the wind just forward of the beam and the helm down to lee. This is heaving to under jib only. Secure the tiller and reef the main. With a double reef in, you'll probably have to tie up the bunt. Re-adjust the tiller to keep the Potter from heading into the wind before you haul the main back up. Once the sail is up, start sailing with the double reefed main. Make sure the centerboard is down which will help to balance the helm as you sail up wind. If that doesn't take out the

lee helm, lower the jib. It's not safe to beat up wind with lee helm in heavy wind. At this point, it's time to seek shelter. With the jib down, you'll have to motor sail to make reasonable progress to windward. These are the tactics you would use in thirty to thirty-five knots of wind. Beyond that point, I think you'll agree that no sail is necessary other than perhaps a jib for down wind sailing if you're going that way. Sometimes in special situations, such as a sudden squall, dropping your jib is the fastest way to reduce sail in such an emergency.

Daysailing is an enjoyable pastime and a major part of pottering. It's the best way to start out when you're new to sailing. As sailing becomes more familiar, you may want to increase your skills and think about some short cruises to places just over the horizon, a little beyond your normal range of daysailing.

4

Going the Distance

Planning

To most people, cruising in a P15 seems ridiculous, but with planning and a sense of adventure it's quite possible. When you consider that you'll only cruise for about two weeks during the year, it's not worth buying a larger boat for cruising when almost all of your time will be spent daysailing. When you think about it, cruising is just a series of daysails strung together. As you cruise, you take one day at a time. Collectively, those days become the cruise. This helps to keep cruising in perspective.

It had been a long hot day of sailing with little wind in the Sea of Cortez, finally ending with two hours of sculling into an anchorage. Looking out the companionway from where I was updating the log book, I could just make out last night's anchorage five miles distant. San Felipe, according to the chart, was still six hundred miles to windward. This cruise suddenly seemed so completely overwhelming. Then, after a moment, I realized that taking one day at a time would eventually change this situation. Somewhere in the days ahead there would be wind and I would get to my destination.

Once you choose to do a cruise, it's up to you to plan it. Your first step will be to develop a rough timeline to frame in your cruise. Using those dates, charts, and tide tables, you begin by checking the tides and currents along your estimated route. This will help give you an idea of what the sailing possibilities will be for that area. You'll also need additional information to continue your planning. This will require a cruising guide which provides information about anchorages and facilities. Choose launching facilities that offer a safe place to store your car and trailer for the length of the cruise. This gives you beginning and ending destinations.

Allowing for tidal currents, choose intermediate destinations along your route that you would enjoy visiting. Extra destinations from the guide will also be needed as alternates.

Because a Potter averages about three knots, ask yourself how much time you want to spend on the water getting to a destination. Those answers will be found on your chart. Using dividers and the mileage scale walk off the distance on your chart between your destinations, if it takes one hour to go three nautical miles in a Potter, how many hours will it take to get where you're going? The answer is found by dividing the total distance by three to find the travel time. When there's an opposing current, you must subtract its speed from the three knots you're sailing, and add in the extra time, but just the opposite is true when the current is with you. From experience you'll find that about four to five hours on the water is about the maximum you'll want to spend. Now, are those distances you've planned between your destinations realistic?

Compromise is always required to do this type of planning. It's better to make the changes on paper now rather than later during the cruise. Imagine trying to put waypoints into your GPS, and make phone calls for reservations while beating down the bay on a breezy afternoon.

Wind is often unpredictable, but it's still a factor in your planning. Because summer storms come and go, and winds and currents don't always work together, it's best to plan layover days. They can be used anywhere they're needed. It also helps to plan for alternative harbors along the way, especially when your destinations are far apart. Having flexibility built into your planning provides safety when unforeseen events occur. If you're new to cruising keep your destinations close together. Alternate your long and short days on the water so you'll remain rested. Use layover days for points of interest or when the weather becomes difficult. Staying at marinas makes cruising in your Potter easier, but anchoring in quiet coves at interesting sights along the way helps to break the monotony.

As you continue to plan, remember, cruising is suppose to be fun and interesting. It's best to keep it that way, so don't become overly concerned about strictly sticking to a planned schedule.

A good thing to do is leave a copy of your cruise plan with someone trustworthy. Stay in contact with that person when you need to make changes to the plan. This way someone will always know where you are.

Equipment

There are many things you'll need to bring along for your cruise. When planning, everything needed will be organized into categories based on a cruisers activities. It will be your responsibility to decide specifically what you'll need to bring for each category.

While in a harbor during a cruise, I couldn't help but notice another Potter skipper beginning to unload his boat behind me. Looking up from my book, I watched him fill his cockpit with all kinds of cruising gear from the cabin. With the cockpit full, he began to transfer everything onto the dock. Curious, I continued to watch, my reading now forgotten. Taking a deep breath, he dove back into the cabin again leaving just his backside exposed. The Potter, now rocking, seemed to be in a tug of war with the skipper over something big. After much banging and bumping, I watched as he gained ground over his unseen adversary. Finally, he slowly backed his way out of the cabin, dragging a big black box. Relative to the little Potter, the box looked like a steamer trunk. Remarking on my observations, I implied that there might be a body inside. Laughing, he opened the box and pulled out a folding bicycle. A few minutes later, the skipper was gone. He had pedaled off to see the sights.

Cruising, which is different than day sailing, requires more equipment. Taking a category approach to it will help make organization easy. The following category headings are based on a cruiser's normal activities. Each is equally important. They are: clothing, sleeping, laundry, showering, food, shelter, mooring, and miscellaneous. You may choose to add on, or adjust these categories as you see fit. However, the object behind this is to limit equipment that's not necessary. Any overloading of the boat will restrict space needed for your own comfort. When that happens you'll find that cruising becomes more difficult than it needs to be.

As you begin to choose what to bring, using a cruisers point of view, is sure to guide you in the right direction. When making a clothing list, your most important objective is to limit your exposure to the elements as you cruise. Using layered clothing that dries quickly is a good choice.

Before sailing off, try sleeping on your boat. If it isn't comfortable, replace or add an additional mattress. Putting a four inch memory foam mattress on top of the regular one works wonders for your comfort.

Experienced cruisers, after arriving at a new marina, always check out the facilities before using them. This helps them learn what's available and answer questions like what it costs to use the shower.

Keep your laundry simple. All you need is a plastic water bottle filled with powdered soap, and some quarters in your laundry bag. This makes doing laundry simple.

The same goes for showering. A small bottle of shampoo, a towel, and some flip flops will meet your basic needs. Bring clothespins to secure your towel, so it can be dried in the cockpit.

Food that's carried in a Potter is usually stored in see through plastic boxes left on an unused bunk for easy access. Water is purchased in easy to pour containers. Cooking is done in the cockpit, with the galley stowed below it. Sealable plastic bags can handle garbage.

The category for shelter is all about cockpit awnings. Sheltering your cockpit from the sun and rain is very important. Design an awning that's quick and easy to set up. Some Potter skippers use flexible battens to support their awnings.

When they're set up, they might remind you of the Conestoga Wagons once seen in the old west.

If the wind comes up, or there's a surge in the harbor, your Potter will need to be well secured so you can get a good night's sleep. At least two fenders and spring lines are needed along with your regular docking lines.

The miscellaneous category covers towels for cleaning up the boat. One other helpful item is a backpack, which is useful for shopping or picnicking. And, for those long hot runs down wind, or if it's raining, an umbrella.

Don't forget your cell phone or VHF. Plans may
change and new reservations will need to be made.

Once you've inventoried, and itemized all your equipment for each category, all that remains is to pack everything in the boat. Try to keep the heavy things in the middle for good hull trim. Just as a hint, many cruisers bring too much equipment. This can affect the performance of the boat, especially when it's poorly stowed.

This is where duffle bags help. They should be medium to large, and easy to grab and close. Number each category on your list. Each duffle should have a numbered identity tag on it that's easy to read. Taking the equipment from the first category, put it in the bag marked number one. Now, if you need anything from the number one category, you'll find it in the bag with same number. One Potter skipper I know uses a boat hook to snag the handles of his duffle bags saving the trouble of crawling into the cabin to find what he wants.

The alternative to the duffle system is to design custom made clothes bags with zippers that hang along the sides of the hull. They're attached to the hull liner and are more than half the length of the bunks. This system could cost more, but can be used anytime, helping to keep clutter out of the cabin whenever the boat is in use.

Keep in mind that the object of all this organization is to have easy access to whatever you need. With proper stowage, it also keeps equipment out of areas that you'll need for your own comfort. Small boats like

Potters need this kind of organization if they're going to be practical for cruising.

Living Aboard in Comfort

Part of being comfortable aboard a Potter, is learning how to move about using the least effort. Most of this will come to you as you gain experience. However, here are some short cuts that will make life easier. When coming aboard, step close to the center of the boat. As you do, you'll notice the boom swing into you, blocking your way. To solve this problem, unshackle your boom vang at the mast, and attach it to the chain plate where the shroud is connected on the side away from the dock. Ease out your mainsheet until the boom moves to the corner of the transom. Secure both your mainsheet and vang, one against the other, locking the boom in place. Now, the next time you come aboard, the boom will be out of the way and you can use it for support as you step aboard.

When going into the cabin, slide from the side bench onto the bridge deck placing your legs in the cabin as you go. Using your arms and legs, move forward onto the center board trunk before lowering yourself inside. The compression post is good to use for pulling yourself forward onto the bunk. Reversing these movements will get you back into the cockpit.

When going onto the foredeck be very careful. The Potter is not as stable as when you're in the cockpit. Move carefully, staying close to the centerline of the boat.

Because you spend so much of your time in the cockpit, make it as comfortable as possible, soft cushions that snap in place along with backrests that pivot and slide on the cockpit rail help a lot. With those improvements, your cockpit will be more comfortable than most larger yachts.

Even when it's raining, you'll spend time in the cockpit with the awning up. It's your front porch. In rain country most awnings are hung under the boom. This is a good approach because it eliminates the opening for the topping lift which will leak. The boom is usually raised high above the deck to allow for sitting head room. Fiberglass battens form half circles secured to the Potter's rails, providing a generous space under the awning. Spinnaker cloth is often used for this type of awning.

This design will keep you dry, which is its main advantage. The awning needs very little space when stowed. It's put in a small stuff bag, and the battens are placed down below alongside the hull. Using a stuff bag keeps the boat dry when the awning is taken down wet, which often happens when leaving early in the morning.

The disadvantage is this awning takes longer to assemble than other designs. It can become quite hot inside on sunny days. Being able to roll the sides of the awning up for ventilation is a real advantage.

If rain is not much of a problem, then you can use an over the boom design. This awning is a canvas rectangle that runs along the length of the boom, and is tied to the mast and topping lift. It's supported by athwartship battens held in pockets under the awning. Lines attached to the batten ends are secured to the cockpit rails to hold the awning in place. There are side flaps that can be pulled down for privacy, or for when it rains. In fair weather they're left up on top of the awning for ventilation.

The advantage of this awning is its adaptability in changing weather. It's made of canvas and is fast to put up or take down even when it's windy. When taken down, it's rolled up on its battens while still on top of the boom and then stowed inside the cabin. When it rains it does leak, because it doesn't fully extend over the cockpit due to the shortness of the boom. Adding back flaps would be an improvement.

Garage sales may also offer other possibilities for awnings. Break down tent poles could be used for making your own awning. One Potter skipper found a pup tent that came within an inch of covering his cockpit, and it worked well with a few modifications.

When selecting cloth for your awning there are several things to keep in mind. Only use light colored cloth. Dark colors absorb heat making it uncomfortable under the awning when the sun is out. Light weight cloth is noisier than heavier cloth because it moves more in the wind. This can be a distraction affecting your ability to sleep on windy nights.

Make your own awning if you have the equipment and skill. If not, have one made. A professional can provide suggestions that will contribute to your design, and build an awning that will last a long time. My awning was first built thirty years ago. Every time I've changed boats, the awning has been modified.

Cooking

For several years I cruised with a disorganized galley. Everything was jammed in under the cockpit and it was always a fight to get out. A plywood board was stowed under the food boxes in the cabin, and served as a table for the stove. It took a lot of time and effort to use this galley, making eating only a momentary pleasure. It was finally decided that something much better was needed to improve this situation.

I began to plan a galley box. Hardly knowing where to start, I built a platform up on the seats to fit flush against the sides and transom of the cockpit. The platform extended a foot and a half forward of the transom giving more than enough room for the planned galley. Using two stainless steel rigging tangs, purchased at the boat store, I bent them into right angles and bolted them to the vertical sides of each cockpit bench. The bent tabs were set flush to the horizontal surfaces of the bench. Next, holes were drilled in the platform above the tangs so it could be bolted down. Taking the platform to the work bench, I built a box on it with three sections. The larger center section held the stove. The other smaller sections on the sides were for dishes, silverware, cooking utensils, and anything else needed for cleanup. The aft portion of the platform, not needed for the box, became open stowage for wet dock lines and fenders. All that was needed now were hatches. These posed several problems. With the tiller in the way, how would the hatches be opened? As it worked out, the port and starboard hatches were hinged on their outboard sides. This allowed them to lean back against the cockpit railings when open. The center hatch sat on runners, just as the Potters main hatch does, and slid forward to be removed. When the galley is in use, the hatch is stowed behind the stove out of the way and used as a wind break. Keeping the galley dry when trailering the Potter in a rain storm was the next problem to solve. Channels had to be built between the hatches to carry off the water. The forward and aft ends of each hatch had a lip that went well below its opening, blocking water from being forced in between the edges by wind. As it turned out this design worked well, keeping the boxes dry inside when trailering at sixty miles an hour in heavy rain.

The final problem was how to lock the hatches so they wouldn't blow open when trailering. This was solved with two barrel bolts. They were fastened horizontally on the rear of each outboard hatch. When locked they kept the center hatch from sliding forward. Because the center hatch couldn't lift, it kept the two side hatches down in place. Modified eye screws were used to lock the barrel bolts in place because they would work open when trailering.

The galley box has now been on several long cruises. It has always remained dry inside, and takes just a few seconds to open for cooking.

Everything I need is right there, but it's never in the way when sailing.

If you decide to build a galley box, make sure that everything you plan to include in it will fit. Build it light to keep the weight down. Mine was built with cedar, one eighth inch plywood and teak trim.

More on Docking

Lying down below in your warm sleeping bag, you try to identify noises in the night. There's the tap, tap, tap, which is probably a halyard, punctuated with a squeak, and then after a moment, a bump. It's the bump that has you worried. Is that something hitting the boat, or maybe it's the other way around? You know that if you don't get up and check, there'll be no sleep. It's about two A.M. as you check your watch with the flashlight. Sticking your head out the hatch your guess proves correct. It's not a good time to be out on the dewy dock in bare feet and boxer shorts, but this is how you learn.

When you come into a harbor after a long sail, securing your Potter correctly will make living aboard more comfortable. There are several things that should be considered. The first is wind direction. When possible, position your boat so the wind holds the boat off the dock. If the wind is blowing parallel to the dock, point your boat into the wind, so your cabin gives better shelter.

A properly tied boat will lie quietly in its berth. When it comes into contact with the dock, the fenders will be where they're needed. To make this happen you'll need two fenders, bow and stern lines, and two spring lines twenty feet long. Without springs, your Potter will surge back and forth against its lines and the dock, when driven by the wind.

After your fenders are down and you've secured both bow and stern lines, put on the spring lines. Tie your spring lines to the loop for the shroud closest to the dock, and lead them fore and aft to their bow and stern dock cleats. If there's wind, tie the windward line first. Tie your fenders off at the widest part of the boat. Secure your spring lines so there's very little fore and aft surge, but not so tight as to pull the Potter up against the dock. Next, adjust the bow and stern lines so the boat is lying parallel to the dock and lands only on its fenders. Give the boat a final test by pushing and pulling it around. Does it always land on its fenders when it bumps the dock? If so, you've passed the test, and should have a good night's sleep.

When your Potter is head to wind, and your lines are set up, you can use the wind to keep the boat off the dock. Go to the bow line and slack it off a little. Notice how the boat falls back against its spring line, and then sails away from the dock on its hull windage. Now that your Potter is clear of the dock, cleat off the bow line. As long as the wind stays on the bow, your boat will remain off the dock. Always try to use the wind to your advantage. Sometimes even small adjustments can make a big difference.

During a storm in Bellingham, Washington, I returned to the dock to find my Potter covered in foam caused by small waves compressed between the hull and the dock. Because of the wind, foam was blown over the boat and back into the cockpit. Just slacking the bow line a few inches solved the problem. As I cleaned the foam off the boat, I glanced back at another Potter behind me. It was now being covered in foam, just as my boat had.

More on Anchoring

The ability to anchor with confidence is something that every skipper earns with experience and dropping your anchor over the side is when your real education starts. Choose out of the way attractive locations with million dollar views when anchoring. Make a picnic of it. Once you've gained experience, try an overnight anchor out. As time goes by, you'll become more at ease with anchoring.

If you're buying an anchor and line for the first time, choose what's recommended by the big box boat store. This will work well in most situations. However, when you begin to do more extended cruising in waters you're not familiar with, you'll want heavier equipment to feel more secure. For instance, a good main anchor for a Potter would be six pounds instead of four. You might consider twenty feet of chain instead of the usual fifteen. Both the line, chain, and anchor all need to be load compatible. At least one hundred feet of line is usually all that's needed, but carrying another rope to increase your scope is a good idea. Bring your original ground tackle along as a back up. You can use it as a stern anchor if space is limited, or to back up the main anchor when it's windy.

You'll soon understand the reasoning for heavier ground tackle when you experience your first squall at night. Once anchored, take bearings on prominent landmarks to check that the anchor is holding. If you've anchored carefully, your Potter won't drag. There's nothing better than missing out on the two A.M. anchor drill in driving rain.

To keep it simple, you only need three pieces of equipment to anchor successfully. These are: your chart, a lead line, and the ground tackle. The chart will show where the sheltered anchorages are and the best bottom to anchor in. For example, let's watch how one skipper anchors.

Just as the late afternoon sun began to set, a small sloop cleared the point and began beating in toward the island anchorage. Interrupting our conversation, I nodded toward the little sloop, and the skipper turned to take it in. We had been sitting in the cockpit of his old yawl talking sailing for some time. The appearance of this small sloop was the first thing that had grabbed our interest all afternoon. Sure, boats had come and gone all day, but mostly large white generic masthead sloops, either decked out for racing or cruising.

However, this little sloop was different, it had a taxi yellow hull with red and yellow sails.

Even at a great distance there was something familiar about the cut of its mainsail, but at the time, I couldn't see well enough to figure out what it was. As it sailed past the first boats at the far end of the anchorage, it didn't seem to get any bigger. In fact it looked smaller as it worked its way through the much larger craft forced to anchor out in deeper more exposed waters. Tacking through the crowded anchorage the little sloop continued on toward us. Now and then, it would become temporarily becalmed, but would tack away toward new cat's paws picking up speed as it went.

"Hey," said the skipper, "Remember when we used to sail like that."

"You know," I said, " That's got to be a P15."

"Well, I can't help wondering what it's doing here,"replied the skipper. "That little yellow boat had to cross at least fifteen miles of open water and that's a real challenge."

In a short while, the Potter skipper sailed by; he nodded his approval of the old yawl by touching the bill of his sailing hat. We waved just as the Potter tacked away, this time toward a shallower part of the anchorage. As he tacked again, we could see he was casting a lead line.

"It looks like we're going to have a new neighbor," I said.

"This will be interesting," the skipper replied, "It isn't often you get to see someone anchor under sail these days. I wonder how he'll do it."

The Potter skipper tacked again, and after a brief distance, came head to wind and dropped his mainsail. As the main was being furled, the breeze drew the Potter around so that it began to sail slowly downwind on its jib.

We did not see what the skipper did next, but we heard the splash of the anchor, followed by the rattle of chain and burr of line running out.

"Don't you think it's a little strange," questioned the skipper, "to anchor by the stern?" "Well it would be," I said, "if it were a big boat, but it makes perfect sense with a Potter."

As the Potter continued to sail slowly down wind under jib, it came to a stop some distance off the yawl's beam. The skipper, aware that his boat had stopped, sat quietly in the cockpit for awhile before checking the tension on his anchor line. Then he casually cast off his jib halyard, using the downhaul to bring the sail to the deck. After putting a harbor furl in both sails, the halyards were secured for the night. Taking a pendant that had been led from the cockpit to the bow and back, he snapped its shackle onto the anchor line, and pulled the pendant to the bow taking the anchor line with it. This turned the Potter head to wind. The anchor line, now running down the side deck from the bow, remained cleated at the stern.

"We'll done!" we yelled. With that, the skipper tipped his cap.

When you use a lead line, stow it in a shallow bucket. Tie the tail of the line to the bail of the bucket. Starting with the tail, coil the line in the bucket. This will leave the lead on top of the coil and handy to grab when needed.

There are lots of ways to cast a lead line. The method you use depends on the conditions you're sailing in. If the winds are light, then you can place one knee on the lee cockpit seat before casting the line forward parallel to your course. If the wind is blowing, luff your mainsail to increase stability and slow the boat, which makes casting the lead easier. When using a motor, cast your lead line on the opposite side from the motor to avoid fouling the propeller and disabling the boat.

The process of casting the lead goes something like this. After connecting the self-steering the skipper picks up the lead and pulls some line out of the bucket. Leaning out on the lee side to keep clear of the hull, he tosses the lead, sending it forward and parallel to the Potter's course. As the lead hits the water, he lets the line run through his casting hand. Just before the Potter passes where the lead went into the water, the slack is taken in. The skipper slides his hand down the line until it touches the water, then he bounces the lead on the bottom to get a feel of what he'll be anchoring in. Keeping his hand on the line, he quickly estimates the distance between his hand and the first fathom mark to reach the surface which is about three feet. Continuing to haul in the lead line, he counts the remaining fathom marks, adding the three feet for a total depth. Having this information helps him determine the amount of scope he'll let out to set the anchor.

For instance, you know that the water you're anchoring in is two and a half fathoms deep, or fifteen feet. The recommended scope for maximum holding power is a ratio of seven to one or one hundred-five feet. However, if you're only anchoring for the afternoon, your experience will tell you using a four to one scope in near calm conditions should work. Using ten fathoms of anchor line, or sixty feet should hold. If it doesn't or the wind comes up you can always let out more scope.

Nothing messes up laying down an anchor faster than a fouled coil of anchor line. This is why it's necessary to keep your ground tackle organized. One skipper keeps his in a plastic rectangular dishpan. The line is coiled clockwise around the edges of the pan, and the chain is piled in the center of the coil. The anchor is secured on top of the line and chain. There's a notch in one end of the pan that holds the anchor's shank, and holes in the sides of the pan to slide the stock through on each side. This secures the anchor in the pan holding the ground tackle in place.

There's a tag at the end of the line showing its length in fathoms. This ground tackle is stowed under the cockpit and is one of many ways to keep your anchor ready for use. This method has proven itself effective and convenient over time.

One of the more puzzling things about an anchorage is seeing boats pointing in all different directions. This usually occurs at the end of each tide when the current is slack, allowing boats to be influenced more by wind. The larger boats are more affected by the remaining current, being deeper in the water, but the smaller ones are more easily blown about until either the current or wind become the more dominant force. When the wind shifts from north to east due to changing weather patterns the whole appearance of the anchorage changes as boats swing to face the east. Boats that were once ahead of you can be alongside and possibly too close for comfort. This possibility needs to be foreseen when you first drop your anchor. Knowing the weather in advance helps to predict these kind of changes.

When inexperienced skippers first anchor, they're anxious about dragging which is normal. They'll nervously watch their boat turn away from the wind first to port, then repeat the process to starboard. This is normal for boats anchored in wind, and is called hunting, or tacking at anchor. Several things cause this. Those boats with more windage up forward are most affected. Boats like Potters, using some chain, but mostly rope will hunt more than other boats using all chain. It's wise to keep this in mind when selecting your location in an anchorage, because larger boats with chain don't swing as much as small boats using rope. This can lead to possible collisions when boats anchor too close. After awhile, you get used to the swinging, and it just becomes part of life on the hook.

Getting underway is usually just the reverse of getting an anchor down. However, there are a few tricks to it that can be helpful. Let's watch the skipper in the yellow Potter as he breaks out the hook.

As we view the anchorage, long shadows are cast across the water as the sun begins to climb into a pale blue sky. The damp morning breeze, what there is of it, is scattered here and there as dark patches on the water. A few people are up and working, taking advantage of last night's dew to wipe the salt from their boats, while others sit in their cockpits taking morning coffee.

The Potter skipper, having finished breakfast, is busy with the last of washing up and stowing for the days sail. Sitting in the cockpit, he scans the sky and anchorage for what the day might bring. While listening to the VHF weather, he reviews the tide and current tables and checks the charts. Finding all to his satisfaction, preparations are made to get underway.

Reaching below for a bucket, he fills it with water from over the side and puts it in the cockpit next to the remaining anchor line. Sitting in the cockpit, the skipper quietly reflects on what's necessary for getting underway. Even though he has done this many times before, he still feels it's important to give it his full attention. Looking up, he checks the halyards, and lays out the jib downhaul so it won't foul when the sail goes up. "All is ready," he thinks, "Let the games begin." Watching the Potter as it hunts to the far left of its anchor, he releases the pendant on the starboard side that holds the anchor line to the bow, and quietly watches as the Potter slowly turns downwind drifting on the breeze until snubbed by its anchor. After removing the pendant from the anchor line, he hauls his boat backwards up toward the anchor. "This is the easy part," he thinks, as he counts the fathoms coming in. Taking his time he washes the mud off the anchor line with the water from the bucket. At the three fathom mark the anchor line is cleated off. The Potter is almost over its anchor. Now, taking a short break, the skipper knows from experience that the real work is about to begin.

What happens next needs to be done quickly and without mistakes. Once the anchor is off the bottom it must be brought aboard quickly, and the jib raised, to control the boat.

When his break is over, the skipper hauls on the anchor line, but suddenly it will come no further. This anchor is well set and difficult to break out. After cleating off the line with tension on it, the skipper moves to the bow of the boat using the boat as a lever to lift the anchor from the soft mud bottom. After standing on the foredeck for a moment, the Potter's bow suddenly drops downward, as the anchor breaks out. It's quickly pulled to the surface. Rapidly plunging the anchor up and down, he washes most of the mud off before it's brought aboard. Once it's aboard the skipper turns his attention to sailing. Raising the jib soon gives the Potter enough speed to maneuver, once the skipper remembers to lower the centerboard.

As he sails past the other anchored boats, he exchanges pleasantries along the way. Apparently, this skipper is a legend at the local yacht club. In a few minutes, the Potter sails clear of the anchorage. The boat is turned into the wind and the mainsail is raised. After heaving to, the skipper washes the mud from the cockpit and stows all the ground tackle. With everything in order, a course is set. The sheets are eased, and with the wind on the quarter, the Potter quickly sails back around the point, slowly disappearing from view out onto a dark blue sea.

If you're new to anchoring, it's easier to anchor under power. Once you become more confident try anchoring under sail. There's nothing like ghosting into a quiet cove and anchoring. It's the best way to finish a day of sailing, and becomes a memory that stays with you.

When cruising, good planning and preparation is the key to success. Keep your Potter and its equipment in good condition. Have a positive attitude and keep your options open. Cruises don't always go as planned. However, a well planned cruise seldom comes to any serious trouble. A successful cruise will become a treasured memory and a source of confidence that you can use to meet many other challenges in life.

5

Pottering About the Race Course

When asking friends why they haven't raced their Potters at events such as the Cruiser Challenge, they often reply, "I've tried, but when I get near the starting line it looks confusing and maybe even dangerous. There are lots of boats all sailing very close together in different directions. Why do they do that?" This point of view is understandable when expressed from skippers who've never raced before.

Let's change that point of view. Come along with me now, as we sail several hundred feet above the race in a magic Potter. This will let you experience everything from a clearer perspective. First we'll have to tweak some more power into the sails; a gust comes, and we have lift off! Of course, rules come with this type of sailing. Once we leave the water we'll be invisible, so there's no use in yelling down to all your friends below.

Speaking of rules, now would be a good time to review the sailing rules of the road. After all, these are the rules being used for the race. There are four of them: Starboard tack has the right of way over port tack when on different tacks. The leeward boat has the right of way over the windward boat when on the same tack. A boat that's being overtaken by another has the right of way. All the boats covered by these rules are obligated not to run into each other.

Getting back to the race, the first thing you notice when you look down is the committee boat. You know this because it's anchored and has flags flying. To further confirm it, you see an orange inflatable buoy about fifty yards off it's side. The space between the buoy and the boat is the starting line. The person who sets the buoy tries to place the starting line at a ninety degree angle to the wind direction. The area downwind from the starting line is called the box and is an imaginary square. It's not marked off, but is considered a restricted area for those boats not starting. Race Committees often use the box to keep things organized when there are different types of boats starting separately.

You now notice that a flag has just been raised on the committee boat. Because you were at the skippers meeting prior to the race, you know the small boats will start in five minutes. The last of the large boats have just cleared the starting line, and the small boats are now entering the starting box. They all begin competing for the best positions on the starting line. The four minute flag on the committee boat is lowered, warning that the start is in one minute. Most of the boats begin to head for the starting line.

The object here is to be the most windward boat and first across the starting line after the horn sounds. Those that are over the line early must circle about and start again. Now all the boats are sailing toward the windward mark. Most are on the starboard tack, while others are sailing on port. Each skipper is looking for the best wind, and advantage over other boats. On this race course all the marks are to be taken to port. That means your boat leaves the buoy on its left side as you round it. As you look ahead, the larger boats are beginning to round the windward mark on the starboard tack with the buoy to port. This gives them the right of way. Once going downwind, mainsails are run out, with jibs poled to the opposite side, catching all the wind possible. The small boats, still beating to the windward mark, are now tacking through the oncoming downwind fleet. This makes things interesting, bringing the sailing rules of the road into play.

After awhile the first of the fleet reaches the lee mark. Marks on the race course are often crowded places and skippers keep a watchful eye to avoid possible collisions. This is always an active time, because at the last minute jibs are brought in and their poles are stowed. Centerboards are lowered and mainsails are sheeted home just as the boats round the mark.

The larger boats now head for the finish line. As you look back, the small boats are closing with the lee mark and about to go through the same maneuvers the larger ones did. Up ahead, the first of the larger boats are finishing.

The race committee records the order of finishes, while sounding a horn for each finisher. Later, at the yacht club, both the skippers and crews have a good time replaying the race, while they wait for the results to be posted. Often dinner is served by the yacht club hosting the event, and an awards presentation is made by the race committee ending the day's activities.

The Game Plan

Now that you've seen a race from a distance, let's develop a game plan that will help when you race. Keeping it simple, a race can be divided into four stages. They are: starting, up wind, down wind, and finishing. The object of your game plan will be to provide strategies for all stages of the coming race. The goal will be to consistently position your boat to advantage within the fleet.

Starting

If you're going to be successful when starting, you need to attend the skippers meeting before the race. The rules for the race are set by the race committee. They'll tell us what the flag signals mean, the course, and the starting time. Other information, such as safety precautions and restrictions will also be covered. The committee will usually stress that this is a fun race and not to be taken too seriously. Taking notes at the meeting will help clear up any confusion you might have once you're out on the water.

The race will begin in an hour, so it's best to start sailing now. You'll have a lot to do before the start. At the skippers' meeting, you learned your course would be a windward leeward one, and that both buoys are visible from the starting line. As you arrive at the line, locate the buoys you'll be sailing around, and tune the Potter for the existing wind conditions. Next, you'll need to check the starting line to see if it's set up perpendicular to the wind direction. This is very important. If it isn't at a right angle to the wind, then one tack will be favored over the other. After sailing both tacks over the starting line, you'll notice that the starboard tack is more perpendicular to the starting line allowing your boat to point closer to the windward mark. If the wind conditions stay the same, you'll start on a starboard tack. Usually a starboard tack is the preferred way to start. Many skippers habitually start that way. Having the right of way is important, but there are times when a wind shift favors the port tack as the best start.

Part of the starting strategy will be to determine how far the Potter will travel in one minute with the existing wind conditions. This will tell how far you need to be from the starting line when the flag is lowered a minute before the start. Timing is everything, because when the starting horn sounds you want to be crossing the line leading the fleet.

Because the larger boats will be starting soon, you must sail clear of the box which is restricted to you now. Once clear of the fleet, and in good view of the committee boat, you heave to and wait for the big boat start. When the starting horn sounds for the larger boats, note the time on your watch, and add five minutes to it. This is the time of your start. The Potter is now sailed back into the starting box close to the one minute position behind the starting line. Keeping a close watch for all traffic, you sail back and forth, sometimes tacking or jibing to avoid other boats. As the race committee lowers the starting flag, your timer is checked. You have one minute before the start. Sails are trimmed in and you head for the line. This is where luck comes in. You have to find openings through the traffic which will lead you to a windward position on the line. The horn sounds and the race is on.

The Windward Leg

You sheet in and cross the line. Checking your position in the fleet, you find your start could have been better. Fifth in a fleet of fifteen P15's leaves room for improvement. The second, third, and forth place boats are to windward. The lead boat is slightly to leeward but well ahead. You have work to do. First you must sail into clear air out from under the boats to windward. If not, the sixth and seventh place boats will soon pass you. Tacking to port, you find yourself rapidly converging with the sixth and seventh place starboard tack boats. As you close with them, a gust lifts your course to windward and your crew shouts excitedly, " We got em!" After passing three boat lengths ahead, you tack over to starboard. Now the boats you've just crossed must take bad air from you or tack away.

Checking your position as you sail finds that you're keeping pace with the second, third, and forth place boats up ahead. The lead boat has slowed with less wind. Looking for more wind, he tacks over to port. A short time later the starboard tack second, third, and fourth place boats cross his bow. Awhile later you hail, "Starboard!" and the once leading boat passes two feet astern of you into fifth place. As a wind shift, known as a header, forces your course to leeward, you tack to port, the course that points closest to the windward mark. The three boats ahead of us have failed to notice this as they race against each other. With every minute that goes by you gain to windward on your rivals. However, you can't stay on the port tack too long because you're approaching the lay line.

The lay line is the final tack that will take you around the windward mark. It takes experience to know just when to tack for the mark. If you tack too soon, you'll be unable to lay the mark. When that happens, you're forced over to a port tack and vulnerable to incoming starboard tackers also rounding the mark. If you tack onto the lay line late, your competitors will gain on the extra distance that you've sailed to get around the mark.

The three leading boats have now tacked over to port and are heading for the lay line. Now, you tack to starboard heading just to windward of the mark. The three port tack boats are rapidly converging on you. It's showdown time. The first two port tackers clear your bow by two boat lengths and tack on top of you, taking your wind. The third place boat, unable to clear you, tacks into your lee, hoping to lay the mark and cut you off.

This is a big gamble for him. If you get a lift allowing you to sail higher, the boat to leeward will cut you off. However, if there's a header, forcing you to sail lower, the leeward boat will be cut off and forced to tack twice to get around the mark. All the skippers on the lay line are betting on the wind they'll need, but that can change at any moment.

For the time being, you're in third place with the fourth place boat in your lee, and are continuing to lose ground to the two lead boats as they take your wind. The first and second place boats round the windward mark. The fourth place boat is unable to lay the mark and must fall back behind you to tack away. Now he threads his way through the other starboard tackers not far behind. You sheet harder, heading up, and just clear the mark by a foot as you round it.

The Leeward Leg

With the whisker pole up and the centerboard raised, the Potter is ready for downwind sailing. You check your position in the fleet. Bad news, the two lead boats have further increased their distance as you were pinching around the mark. More bad news, there's a boat behind you that has gained and will take your wind if you don't defend yourself. Moving off to one side, you sail out of the following boats wind shadow.

At this point, you begin planning your strategy to the leeward mark. Remembering that the wind was stronger on the right side of the course, you choose to pass the restricted starting line on your starboard side. This is a big gamble, but you're hoping that the wind will still be there. Once past the starting line, you'll jibe over to a starboard tack giving you the right of way as you enter the fleet again, near the lee mark. The downside of this is that you'll have to jibe again at the lee mark as you round it to port. The lead Potters have chosen a course to the other side of the starting line. Meanwhile, the rest of the fleet have decided to follow them. The pressure is on! Right now you need some magic. Will this strategy work? If it does, you'll get another shot at those lead Potters. If it doesn't, your third place will probably evaporate into fourth or fifth place.

You've gained on the lead Potters, but so has the rest of the fleet. It looks like it's going to be very crowded at the lee mark. Jibing onto a starboard tack after passing outside of the starting line, you begin to close with the fleet sailing toward the lee mark. Just before you move into the fleet the whisker pole is taken down and the board is lowered so you can maneuver. Boats give way as you hail starboard. Some, caught by surprise, are forced to jibe over. As you cross in front of one Potter, its skipper attempts to slip between you and the mark. You quickly jibe over and cut him off, sheeting in as the mark sweeps by. With the leeward mark behind you now, you check your position and find you're still in third place with the two lead Potters less than two boat lengths ahead.

The Finish Line

Throughout this race you've been using offensive tactics. But with more than half the race over, it seems unlikely you'll be able to catch the two lead boats. Holding the fourth place boat in check, and settling for a third place finish seems like the safest option in the first race of a three race series.

Just as you finish thinking this strategy through, the fourth place boat tacks over to starboard and so do you. The number four boat continues to lose ground as you take his air. Discouraged, he begins to focus on the two boats behind him, tacking to port again in an effort to cover them, while evading your wind shadow. A moment later you also tack to port, continuing to cover the boats in your lee, keeping yourself between them and the finish line.

Meanwhile, the two lead boats have broken off their tacking duel. The lead boat, the one with red and green trim, having gained on the second place boat, is now on the port tack, the same as you.

He's to windward of your position and a difficult one to catch. The second place boat continues on the starboard tack, hunting for more wind, hoping to make up for his loss.

A few minutes later, the number two boat also tacks back over to port after losing ground to us. Now we are all to the left side of the finish line. The lead boat tacks over to starboard, his lay line to the finish, and well ahead of the second place boat. As you reach the lay line, you also tack to starboard. The second place boat, tacks with us to starboard heading for the finish line. "This looks close," your crew says quietly. As we come to the finish, there's a beep, beep, as the horn sounds for both the second and third place boats.

The race is over. "Well what do you think?" you ask your crew. " It's too close to call," he says thoughtfully. "I guess we'll just have to wait for the results posted back at the yacht club."

Using What You Have

Like most of us, when I was a boy, just starting out in sailing, I had to make do with what I had. My sail was made of Egyptian cotton. There were several small holes in it covered with blue iron on patches that my mother put on. It was easy to spot me at a regatta. I always stood out. No one used cotton sails anymore. Over time, I was able to improve my situation somewhat. After working on larger yachts, I saved enough to purchase a sloop. It was a great boat, in good condition, with better sails than I had before. The sails however, were made of Orlon, a forerunner to Dacron, the preferred material. You could hear the wind pass right through those Orlon sails when a gust filled them. When the wind blew hard when racing, we did well. Thanks to the wind, and Dave, my ever faithful crew, we were in the upper half of a large competitive fleet. However, when it wasn't windy, we just had to make do and sail the best we could.

After purchasing a new P15, many decades later, I promised myself there would be no more making do. The making do days are far behind me now, but through that process, I've learned what it takes to get the best out of a boat on a limited budget.

Making What You Have Work

To race a boat successfully, everything must work well. Sails need to run up and down smoothly. All lines need to lead fair, as they move through their blocks, and be easily secured with reliable cleats. The up and down motion of the centerboard and rudder blade also need to operate easily under sail. Most of this can be achieved through adjustments and maintenance.

If the boat is to perform well, other basic items, sometimes missing, will need to be aboard. They are: a hiking stick, whisker pole, and boom vang.

Sails

The quality of your sails is very important when racing. When air flows over a sail's surface and is disrupted by wrinkles or a fluttering leech, it's performance is affected. Often wrinkles can be avoided just by properly tensioning the sails.

The full length top batten of the Potter's mainsail controls the shape of the upper part of the sail, and supports its roach. If the top batten is overly thick, the upper part of the sail will be too flat. When the batten is too thin, the top will not only be very full, but the roach will sag in toward the luff, creating wrinkles at the forward ends of the lower batten pockets. This is known as batten poke making for a slow sail. To solve this, change the upper batten so it allows the sail to be fuller, but strong enough to support the roach of the sail, keeping it from sagging in toward the luff. The top batten should have a constant curve with its deepest part midway from the luff to the leech of the sail. The next time you're sailing, check your upper batten; if it isn't right, experiment with the batten pocket tension, or use different battens until your sail sets better. Sailmakers sell fiberglass battens, but they're easy to make out of hardwood if you can use a table saw.

Mast Rake

Mast rake refers to the angle your mast is tilted aft. Having the correct aft rake helps your Potter perform better upwind. However, aft rake is slow when reaching or running. Because Potters sail with fixed masts, you must choose the best possible rake for all points of sailing.

To check mast rake, put your Potter on a flat surface. Use the wheel jack on the trailer to level the boat fore and aft. Once the mast is up, use the jib halyard as forward support for the mast. Pull the main halyard down until it almost touches the cabin top. Then adjust your jib halyard until the hanging main halyard lands about six inches aft of the mast on the cabin top. This is a good starting place. Using a helper to hold the mast steady, adjust your jib stay and shrouds so they're set with equal tension. Make a note of this setting for future reference.

Check the results by sailing with other Potters on all points of sail. If your boat is slow running or reaching, decrease the amount of rake. When it's slow beating, increase the amount of rake using your adjusters one hole at a time. This is a trial and error process that skippers must go through as they tune their boats.

Jib Sheet Leads

Because mast rake changes your jib sheet leads, it's best to check them. Both the foot and leech tension on your jib should be equal, with the jib sheet generally bisecting the angle of the clew. On the standard Potter, the jib sheet leads are not adjustable. However, there's a way around that. You can move your jib up or down the jib stay to change the sheeting angle. All you need to do is adjust the length of the jib tack pendant. This is the line that fastens your jib to the deck at the bow. When you tack, turning into the wind, the jib should luff evenly from top to bottom with the sheet leads properly adjusted. Another way of checking this to is to use the telltales on the jib. They should all flow horizontally when the jib leads are set correctly on a beat. If you are using inside sheeting, the jib leads are set with the barber haulers. When jib leads are correctly set, your boat will point better and sail faster.

Organize Your Sailing

Because it takes energy to race a boat well, teach yourself the easiest way to do things. This isn't hard to do, it just takes some discipline on your part. Once you get the routine down, you'll find setting up the boat and racing it will be much easier.

Develop a routine for each sailing maneuver, such as tacking, jibing, and putting up the whisker pole. Just organize each task, breaking it down into a step by step process. Memorize the steps and train yourself to follow through on them. This probably will seem excessive, until you experience the results. Once you get it down, your sailing will improve, especially in rough conditions, when it's very easy to make mistakes.

On board a boat, everything has its place. Stow everything in your Potter where it needs to be and keep it that way. This helps make sailing so much easier.

Handling the Jib

Sometimes jibs can create problems. Here are three suggestions that will make handling your jib easier. Use a toggle to release your jib sheets from the sail.

Leave the sheets on deck full time. This will make it easier to change or fold a jib. When you fold your jib, do it in a way that will expose the jib hanks, making it easier and faster to rig. If you have more than one jib stowed in a bag, mark them so it's easier find the one you need.

I'm sure there are many different ways of doing things that will help keep your racing simple. I leave it to you to develop your own sailing style and see how many tricks you can discover for yourself. This activity is one of the most rewarding parts of sailing.

Attitude

Many things happen on the race course. Some of these have to do with changing sailing conditions. At times, problems are created by those you're competing with. Problems are part of sailboat racing and it's up to you to foresee and solve them the best way you can.

Most of us that sail remember our first race. It was the one that first ranked our sailing ability among our peers. That experience for me was being second to last in a thirty five boat fleet. Results like that leave you with a choice. You can say I'm no good at this, or I can do better.

Using a positive attitude, one that allows you to think a problem through clearly, will give the best results. To do this when racing, you must distance yourself emotionally from the race, not only as you sail in it, but also from its final outcome as well. Take all that competitive energy you use during the race and focus it on sail trim and helmsmanship rather than your competitors.

When skippers who sail small boats come together, information is often exchanged and friendships become possible. Racing provides many opportunities for this.

Here's an example. Now that the day's racing is over, you think it's a good idea to get off the boat and stretch your legs a bit. It's always fun to walk around and look at boats in the harbor. While walking, you find your thoughts interrupted by people talking and laughing. As you glance down the dock, you see people sitting around in folding chairs, blocking part of the dock near a fleet of moored Potters. As you get closer, many in the group invite you over. To them, it doesn't seem to matter that you didn't bring a snack for sharing, but if you sail, you've got something to offer. After introductions are made, you're asked how you did in the race, and in a short time find yourself in the middle of the conversation and having a good time.

My first three years of sailing and racing were restricted to small lakes. My sailing friends soon realized I was serious about racing, and provided opportunities for me to crew on different boats. Racing on other boats in serious competition was like going back to sailing school all over again. I was learning a lot. If I hadn't raced my little boat, those crewing opportunities probably wouldn't have come my way so soon.

Back then, we were a racing family. My brother and I raced ten foot catboats and my father a twenty foot sloop. When the weekend of racing was over we would talk about it after dinner. Spoons would become boats, salt and pepper shakers would be marks, and a random knife would signal wind direction. The discussions were lively, covering tactics and racing rules.

Later, even when not racing, those skills have remained. Because of racing, we all became better sailors. If the motor didn't start, we could sail back without it, and right onto the trailer if necessary. Our boats were well rigged and tuned. We wouldn't have it any other way. When other boats got near, we would always do our best to out sail them. Why? Because once upon a time, we were racers.

Racing is a lot of fun. Even so, it's not a top priority with many Potter skippers. Potters were never designed with racing in mind, but that doesn't mean they aren't raced. Races are often included in pocket cruiser activities. Also, there's always a little racing going on, even when cruising in a group from one place to another. It's called fox and hounds. Racing is just one more of many enjoyable activities a skipper can choose to do while having fun with his Potter.

6

Hot Rodding a Potter

In chapter five, we've discussed using what you have to be successful when racing. That just covered the basics.

Now, it's time to take your Potter to the next level, not only for racing, but just for the pleasure of sailing. You'll find it's much more fun to sail a P15 that points higher, and sails faster than it ever has before. Also, tacking and jibing will be easier, and the boat will be safer to sail. I know this is a very tall order to meet, but I've been sailing my Potter that way for years. The changes I'm about to suggest are the best of over forty modifications that are now in use aboard my Potter.

Inside Sheeting

First on the menu of changes will be sheeting your jib inside the shrouds, and using barber haulers. This is a big step to take, but the windward performance and ease of handling is worth it, even though it requires extra equipment and effort on your part to install. Before you start, you'll need to be convinced this is right for you.

The next time you rig your Potter for sailing, when the wind is light, lead your jib sheets inside your shrouds. While sailing on the wind, use your hand to lead your jib sheet up to the aft corner of the cabin top. Just this simple action should suggest some of the possibilities that inside sheeting can offer. The jib sheeted inside the shrouds will have a slightly rounded foot and point a little higher than it would when using the standard sheeting angle.

However, when you begin to reach or run, you can't help but notice how the lee shroud fouls the jib sheet once it's eased. This is where barber haulers come in. A barber hauler's job is to control the shape of the jib by adjusting the jib's sheet lead. To demonstrate this, take a small line and loosely tie a bowline around your jib sheet between the sail and where you're holding it on the cabin top. Lead it down to where your shroud is attached and back through that loop to the cockpit. What you've just made is a make-shift barber hauler for use off the wind.

If you're reaching with inside sheeting, use the barber hauler to pull the jib sheet down to cabin top level. This is generally about the best sheeting angle for the jib on that point of sail. Notice how the leech of the jib is not twisted way off at the top losing power, and the jib sheet is barely touching the shroud. Now release the barber hauler and move the sheet outside the shroud to its standard lead. Look at how the jib sets with standard sheeting while reaching. Is there still a lot of twist off at the top, forcing you to over sheet the jib? Which sheeting angle would you choose, inside the shroud with the barber hauler, or outside with the standard sheeting angle and no barber hauler?

When running, pull the barber hauler down to the deck. This will eliminate fouling the jib sheet against the shroud. Leading the sheet there will also hold your whisker pole steady, not allowing it to lift in the gusts and spill wind. Even if you don't use a whisker pole downwind, the jib will be less likely to jibe back and forth when winged out with the sheet led forward at deck level giving more control.

Inside sheeting on a Potter is much easier to use. There's less friction when hauling in the jib as you tack because the sheets no longer travel around the shrouds. You also have less sheet to pull in because there's less distance for the jib to travel from one tack to the next. Because the cam cleat is up higher on the cabin top, you can pull down as you sheet in the jib. This downward pull leads the jib sheet into the cam, holding it in place so you can slide your hand back up the sheet for a final pull. Even when it's blowing hard, tacking still only takes one hand. When tacking you don't shift your weight as far to leeward as you would when using the standard sheeting position. All this becomes even easier when you use a jib sheet cam that swivels. When sailing with a crew, the cabin top jib cam is more accessible, even when the crew leans back against the cabin. When putting up the pole, it's much easier to adjust your sheets from the companionway with the jib cams on the cabin top.

Inside sheeting requires using two barber haulers for each side. The inboard barber hauler on the cabin top adjusts the jib sheet lead when beating. As you reach or run, the outboard barber hauler with its cam cleat on the cockpit combing will move the jib sheet lead forward and outboard where it belongs for those points of sail. If you're sailing on a broad beat or a close reach, either barber hauler can be used. The systems overlap. When not in use, the barber haulers just run free taking care of themselves.

Rigging Barber Haulers

Setting up inside sheeting with barber haulers is not difficult. The new jib sheet cams will be located near the outboard aft corners on the cabin top.

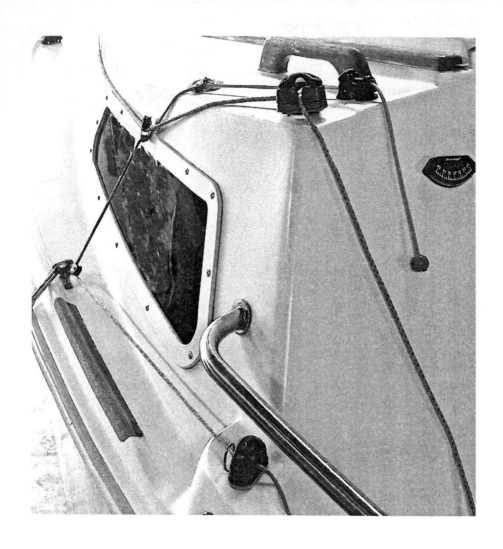

The barber hauler cams for beating are also placed on the cabin top inboard of the jib cams. Eye straps for the barber haulers, with small blocks on them, are fastened one foot forward of the new jib sheet cams.

The outboard barber hauler blocks for reaching and running are fastened to the chain plate loops at deck level. Use your old jib sheet cams for the outboard barber hauler cams if they work.

About sixteen feet of one eighth inch line is needed for all the barber haulers on the boat. The lines will lead out of both the inboard and outboard barber hauler cams on each side of the boat through the two small blocks, one at the chain plate and one at the eye strap on the cabin top. The lines are then tied to a common block riding on each of the jib sheets between the cam and the sail. Before starting this project, it's a good idea to review maintenance and improvements, in chapter one. This will help get you started off on the right foot.

Using Barber Haulers

Beating

As I mentioned, the inboard barber haulers on the cabin top are only used when beating. There are two reasons for using them. The first is to adjust the sheeting angle of the jib sheet so the jib telltales to fly horizontally as you sail up wind. The second is to bring the leech of the jib in to parallel the leeward curve of the mainsail as much as possible.

Air that moves along the lee side of the sails is the main driving force for the boat. When that air moves aft on the jib, it needs to continue uninterrupted as it transfers onto the lee surface of the mainsail. To help make that happen, the barber hauler and jib sheet must work together. Proper adjustment will give better performance than the two sails would have if working individually. Be careful not to over trim the barber haulers. Once the barber haulers are set, they don't have to be adjusted unless wind and water conditions change noticeably.

As sailing conditions change, your Potter must adapt to them. Here are some general guide lines. In very light air you will not need barber haulers because upper sail twist helps performance. As the wind pressure on the sails increases, it will twist the leech of the jib out farther, no longer paralleling the lee side of the mainsail. Use the barber hauler to correct this. When the wind gets to the point where you can no longer hold the boat down, let the barber hauler off. The leech of the sail will twist off, dumping air from the upper part of the jib helping to reduce heeling. This will open the slot between the jib and main allowing room for the mainsail to also be eased for balancing the helm and to reduce heeling.

Reaching

When sailing with the wind on the beam, the inboard barber hauler is no longer used. Free it before using the outside one. Bring the outboard barber hauler in until the jib sheet is pulled down to about cabin top level.

Check all the jib telltales on the lee side of the jib. They must stream horizontally. The windward telltales are probably not working because they're in the lee of the jib's luff. Ignore them when reaching. Once the barber hauler has set the telltales, use the jib sheet for fine tuning. Usually, holding the boat down on a reach is not a problem, but when it is, the barber hauler can be eased to limit heeling.

Running

Barber haulers are very easy to use on this point of sail. Using the outboard barber hauler, just pull the jib sheet down to deck level.

This avoids chaffing the sheets on the shroud and
stabilizes the jib. Sometimes when it's very windy,
you'll be unable to set your whisker pole when sailing
alone. However, this won't stop you from winging the
jib out. Your jib will be more stable, and less likely to
jibe back and forth with the barber hauler full on.
When the whisker pole is up, the barber hauler plays

an important role as it's downhaul. This is especially true in temporary situations that demand reaching with the pole up.

Be careful not to over trim the barber haulers, which is like putting on the brakes. Potters thrive on some upper sail twist. Anytime you trim the barber hauler for different wind conditions, check the jib sheet trim as well.

The Fixed Traveler

Each time you make a change to a system, something else is affected, and that's the case here. When a jib's sheeting angle is moved closer to the boat's center line, the mainsail is also affected. It too must be sheeted closer. This is difficult with a standard rope traveler. When you sheet harder to avoid the jib from back winding the mainsail, the mainsail's leech closes, increasing weather helm. So, as you attempt to overcome the backwinding of the main, another problem is created. Using a fixed traveler solves this problem by pulling in the mainsail farther, but with much less tension on the leech.

Looking at racing boats, we find that the mainsheet car that slides on the traveler track is pulled to windward in light air. This helps create the twist needed for the mainsail in those conditions. In moderate breezes, the car is centered, but let down to leeward in heavy air to reduce weather helm when necessary. This is how racers on larger boats control their mainsails. We can do almost the same thing without using their expensive travelers.

Ah Tiller the Fun, the Potter that I sail, has a rope traveler with its sheet block fixed in the centered position. Here's how it works. In very light air, the mainsheet tensions the traveler only from its windward side. Its lee side is slack. This is best in light air because it opens the leech. As the wind increases, you sheet harder to close the mainsail's leech, and develop more power for those conditions. Sheeting harder increases overall tension on the traveler, centering its pull. It also tensions the jib stay, allowing the boat to point higher. When the wind is heavy, the mainsheet must be eased to reduce power and balance the helm. Any excessive mainsail twist due to easing the sheet from its centered position can be reduced by using boom vang tension. Racing boats also use this tactic once their booms are outboard of their travelers.

Making a Fixed Traveler

The quickest way to make a centered traveler is to modify your old one. Take your traveler off the boat. Double it with the traveler block in the part that bends back on itself. Holding the block in that position, and using both parts of the doubled traveler, tie an overhand knot just below the block securing it in the loop. You could also use a ring with the traveler spliced to it as an alternative.

The Jib Sheet Toggle

If your boat is rigged with inside sheeting and barber haulers, you may already know that it takes a little extra time to rig your jib sheets. There's a way around that. In fact, using a toggle on your jib sheets, makes rigging the jib faster than the standard method of reeving the sheets. With the toggle, you won't have to remove your jib sheets. They can stay on deck. Put them over the bow cleat, and sheet in the slack with the jib cams and barber haulers to secure them.

My first impression of the toggle was that it probably wouldn't hold up, but in fact, it has worked very well. Even in heavy winds, it doesn't come off.

Making a Toggle

To make a toggle for the Potter, the jib sheets need to be no larger than a quarter of an inch in diameter and a single piece of line twenty six feet long. The jib's clew grommet should have a hole width of five eighths of an inch to receive the jib sheets and toggle. If your grommet and jib sheets have different dimensions, make your pattern fit what you have.

You should use a small piece of wood as a pattern to find the thickness needed for the toggle. The pattern must fit through the grommet with the jib sheet bent over its end, and running along both its sides. To work in this case, it will probably be about a half inch high and a little less than a quarter inch thick. When you're able to pass the pattern and the jib sheets through the grommet, the pattern will have the thickness needed to make the toggle.

Now take a larger piece of hardwood the same thickness as your pattern. Drill a hole just large enough to thread the jib sheet through it. The next step is to shape the toggle around the hole. The grain in the hardwood must run lengthwise. The toggle is two inches long with the hole in the center. The upper edge is cut down to a sixteenth of an inch above the hole and is shaped in a curve down to its lower corners. The lower length is then trimmed so the toggle just fits through the jib grommet. When finished, the toggle will look like the profile of a quarter round with the centered hole a sixteenth of an inch below its upper edge.

Smooth up all the edges with sandpaper. Thread the
toggle onto the jib sheet and center it. Using the
doubled sheet, tie an overhand knot about four

inches below the toggle. The toggle should be in the loop and secured by the knot.

Use the toggle to thread the sheets through the jib's clew grommet. Turn the toggle so the maximum amount of wood is between the sheet and the jib. It's not necessary to remove the toggle if the sheets are twisted, just rotate the toggle.

The Whisker Pole

If you've adapted your jib sheets to use the quick release toggle, they may no longer work with your existing whisker pole. There are two ways you can approach this problem. One way is to just change the end of your existing pole to work with the new jib sheet modification. That will take fitting stainless steel tangs on your whisker pole for gripping the jib sheets.

The other way of dealing with the whisker pole is to start from scratch. It's not difficult to find the materials you need for a new whisker pole at both the local hardware and boat store.

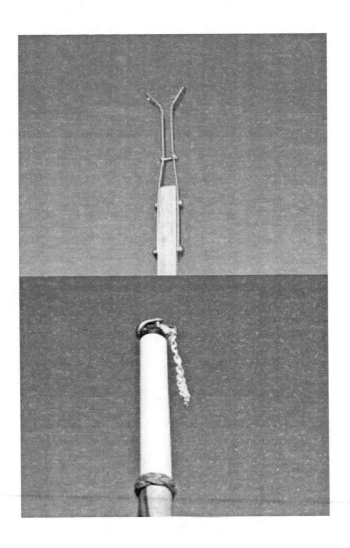

My whisker pole was made from a window washing pole. I used a piece of plastic pipe to fit over the end of the pole and a plastic spinnaker pole end fitting to fit inside the pipe. The stainless tangs, found in the rigging section of the boat store, were bolted onto the other end of the tapered pole and bent to grip the sheets. Your pole should be long enough to pull the jib out flat, holding the sail perpendicular to the center line of the boat. Position the pad eye on the mast so the pole is horizontal when pulled full back.

Changing your whisker pole is a worthwhile project. Using a pole with tangs will make winging out your jib and jibing it much faster than using the conventional clip on pole. With this system, the pole stays connected to the jib sheets during the jibe. This pole also floats when accidentally dropped over the side.

The Cunningham

When the water is flat, and the wind is moderate, a Potter's mainsail will carry its draft at almost fifty percent aft of its luff. With main sheet tension, the leech of the sail is almost closed. This sail trim works well for those conditions. However, as the wind builds and you begin to have difficulty with weather helm and holding your Potter down, the draft of the sail needs to be moved forward to open the leech.

This is what a Cunningham does. All you have to do is pull one line, to accomplish this. Even when not racing, the Cunningham makes your Potter safer, giving you more control over heeling and weather helm.

To rig one, a sailmaker puts a grommet in your sail next to the luff about seven inches above the tack. A three to one tackle is used for tensioning the luff of your mainsail, and is led back to a cabin top cam cleat.

My first thought on the Cunningham,was why not use the downhaul? As I tried this, I found it difficult to slide the boom down the mast to tension the luff. Then I tried the main halyard, but both methods required using both hands while the boat continued on under sail. The Cunningham, however, easily tensions the luff from above the boom and releases it when not needed for running or reaching with one hand as you sit in the cockpit. Because the adjustment is easy to do, it's often used for shaping the mainsail to control heeling and weather helm as the wind increases.

A good example of this would be after beating around a point in a good breeze, you slack the sheets, then ease the Cunningham off to power up the mainsail again as you reach toward the harbor.

Even though the Cunningham moves the draft forward in the mainsail, it can only move the draft that's put in the sail by the outhaul. Each are separate systems, but work together when shaping the sail.

The Adjustable Outhaul

There are often times when you must adjust the draft in your mainsail while underway. You should be able to do this on any point of sail with one hand. To power up a sail, you increase its draft. When you can no longer hold the boat down, then the sail must be flattened to reduce power and maintain control. Having an adjustable outhaul is important, not just for speed, but also for safety.

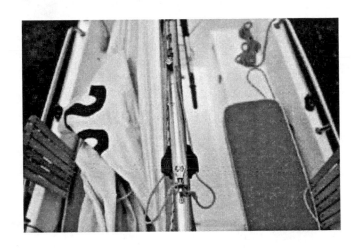

To make this possible, a small four to one tackle will need to be attached to your outhaul line. Make sure you use minimum stretch line for your outhaul. If you rig your outhaul tackle so it's double ended, it can lead through a cam cleat on each side of the boom. This way draft can be controlled from either tack. Locate the cam cleats about three and a half feet aft of the boom's gooseneck. This will put them within easy reach of your sailing position in the cockpit. Even while running, the outhaul will still be accessible from the hatchway.

Tie a stopper knot in the outhaul line. Position the stopper knot so the draft in the mainsail is about seven inches out from the boom with the outhaul free. This is the draft the mainsail needs when reaching. Now, all you have to do is free the outhaul to get the proper draft for reaching.

The Clew Downhaul

At the aft end of the boom is the clew downhaul. This is a small piece of line that is led through the mainsail clew grommet around the boom and secured to itself. Beads, the kind you would use for macramé, are threaded onto it and held in place with stopper knots. This allows the clew downhaul to move along the boom without binding while the draft of the mainsail is being adjusted.

Without the clew downhaul, the outhaul doesn't work. As you attempt to increase the draft in the mainsail without the clew downhaul, the boom just falls away from the sail leaving the boom hanging with little change in draft.

As you use the outhaul when beating, note where the aft tackle block is along the boom. When the boat is performing well, mark it's position on the boom so it will serve as a benchmark for future adjustments.

The Mainsheet Cam

There's always some discussion about where to put the mainsheet cam cleat. It's location is often varied, because most skippers select a location that they're comfortable with. Others just use what's on the boat. Mine is located on the boom. It has been moved at least three times and at one point, was double ended so it could be used from either the cam on the traveler or a cam on the boom. It finally found a permanent home three feet seven inches aft of the gooseneck on the boom. That location gives easy access through all points of sailing. Some mainsheet cams are reversible. This means you have a choice to pull aft or forward when freeing the sheet from the cam. Pulling forward to free the sheet works best on all points of sail. If you choose to free the sheet by pulling aft, it will become more difficult to release when reaching or running. The part of the mainsheet not being used is left in the cabin on the port bunk out of the way. It's not under foot and is free to run when needed.

No matter where you place your mainsheet cam, if it takes much more than two seconds to free the mainsheet, then its location can be a safety issue.

Imagine as you sail your Potter that a strong gust is about to strike the boat. Can you reach your mainsheet in time? Is the position of your cam cleat usable on any point of sail, even when tacking or putting up the whisker pole?

The Hiking Board and Strap

Using your weight to limit the angle of heel is called hiking out. You don't often see Potter skippers do that. Perhaps they've never sailed in small boats, or find the idea just a bit too challenging. However, hiking when it's breezy is just part of hot rodding your Potter. If you have the proper equipment for it, hiking is not a problem. In fact, it's more comfortable than sitting in the cockpit.

The hiking bench you sit on rotates under you so you're always upright. It's the Potter that heels. You're probably wondering how you could possibly feel secure up there teetering around on a little seat.

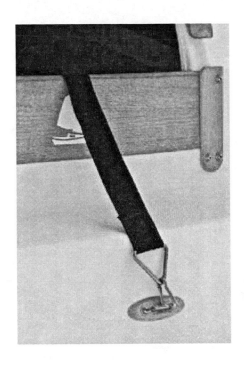

Well, you couldn't, unless your feet were tucked under a webbed hiking strap, the same kind you use to winch your boat up onto it's trailer. Being up that high on the rail keeps you away from the spray, and provides a good view of the sails.

However, there's a blind spot behind your jib that you'll need to see around to be safe. This is how it's done. Lean aft while heading the boat up to see what's behind the jib. Then lean forward while bearing away from the wind to visually cover the rest of the blind spot.

Up in Desolation Sound, during a rising gale, I was beating toward shelter when a wave broke over the foredeck throwing the Potter sideways down the face of the wave into the trough. It was a wild ride. Using the strap and hiking bench allowed me to throw my weight against the violent motion to leeward, keeping me balanced and still in the boat. Had I been sitting in the cockpit I possibly could have been thrown off the seat to leeward.

Making a Hiking Strap

Installing a hiking strap is a fun project. First cut a board that will fit into your lower hatchway the same size as the smaller of your existing hatch boards. The board's purpose is to lift the strap so you can slide your foot under it as you move to the rail. Next you'll need two identical pad eyes. They're fastened back to back, so just get the nuts and bolts for one. The first pad eye is placed outside, just above center, in the sloped forward end of the footwell. After drilling the holes for it, the second pad eye is used as a backing on the inside. Bolt the two together. Now you'll need a two inch wide webbed strap, three feet long and two D rings. These items are found at the boat store. Sew the strap over metal D rings on each end.

A sailmaker can do this for you in a few minutes. The D rings will serve to connect other attachments. Put a snap shackle on one D ring, and fasten it to the pad eye in the cockpit.

The hiking strap is then run forward over the hatch board into the cabin and down to the inside pad eye. That end of the strap will be permanently attached to the inside pad eye with a line that can be adjusted. Even when the hiking strap is set up and not being used, you'll find it's never in the way. The hatch board holding the strap up should not come out when the strap is in place. You can stow the strap on a hook in the cabin, and the board can be stowed in the bin aft of the bunk when you need to put your existing hatch boards back in place.

The Hiking Boards

These will serve as comfortable back rests most of the time. The hiking boards rotate on the cockpit rails. They also can be slid fore and aft as needed for comfort. When you want to hike out, slide your foot under the hiking strap first, and then move up onto the hiking bench. It will rotate up under you and become a comfortable seat on the rail. Once there, as I said before, you'll remain level as the boat rotates under you.

If it's not possible for you to build your own hiking boards, then call on a professional for help. The hiking boards are worth it. All you need is this book with its pictures and basic measurements to complete the project.

When building a hiking board, use any scraps of wood to create the patterns for the project. The four pieces used to make the frame are twelve by one and a quarter by five eighths inches. They are mortised together using a table saw. The vertical pieces are spaced four and one half inches apart and are centered on the twelve inch horizontal pieces which support the slats that you rest on. The point of rotation on the vertical frame is three inches down from the top of the horizontal frame to the center of the Potter's rail. The hiking board is fastened to the rail with two chocks and four screws. Be sure to drill the one inch pivot holes before assembling the frame. Some file work may be necessary so they freely rotate on the rail.

You can make the slats for the hiking board to your own design, or copy the ones in the picture. Be sure to include a gentle curve to the inboard edges of the horizontal pieces where the slats are fastened.

This is for your comfort. The slats are one eighth inch thick, except for the two outside ones which lack support and are three sixteenths of an inch. The bottom of the horizontal frame has a rounded piece added to support the bench as it lands anywhere along the combing when the bench is in the upright position. Teak is the best wood to use for this project. It matches the trim on your Potter, and is easy to maintain when left unfinished. Just wash the hiking boards down with the boat.

7

Pulling it All Together

As you know, books are organized into paragraphs and chapters with each sailing subject covered within that framework.

However, a sailor's way of understanding those sailing subjects works differently. When sailing, they mentally move across paragraphs, chapters, and even books, randomly connecting needed information on related subjects to help them sail successfully.

Often an author is restricted by organizational structure and can only imply related information within that given framework. Because of that, this chapter will attempt to show how interconnected subjects work together for an overall improvement in sailing performance on any boat, plus a few new subjects, sails and sailing alternatives. This hopefully will be the glue that brings everything together into what is known as "The Gentle Art of Pottering."

A Sailing Boat and the Relationship of its Systems

The parts and pieces that go together to create a sailboat are related. These pieces, organized into various systems, achieve particular functions aboard the boat. Sometimes it takes several systems working together to accomplish a task. Keeping in mind that a small sailboat's goal is to use the wind as its source of power, it becomes necessary for most of those systems to control the sails. The skills needed to work those systems are known as sail trim and are part of a skipper's helmsmanship.

Helmsmanship

There are many skills that add up to good helmsmanship. Mastering those skills will result in sailing your Potter efficiently along the shortest route toward a selected destination. As you sail along that course, telltales are read correctly, sails are shaped and trimmed for both wind and water and a course is set on the tack pointing closest to your intended destination. It's the active coordination of all those skills that define good helmsmanship.

The Helmsmanship of the Lifted Tack

As a lift comes, you head up, following that wind shift to windward, bringing the boat's course closer to its destination. When a header forces your course to leeward, away from that destination, it's time to tack. The new tack provides the lift you'll need to continue pointing closer to your destination. As a good helmsman, you always sail the lifted tack. It's the shortest route to your destination.

To help you better understand this, hold your thumb and forefinger at a ninety degree angle to each other. Put some object marking your destination at an equal distance between the tips of your thumb and forefinger. Now pretend that your thumb and forefinger are boats, each sailing on opposite tacks. As you bring your finger toward that destination your thumb moves away from it. This is what happens when the wind shifts giving your imaginary "finger boat" the advantage of sailing closer to its

destination. That boat, pointing closer, is sailing in a lift. The other "thumb boat" on the opposite tack, is sailing in a header. It is now forced away from its destination and must come about to the other tack to gain the advantage again. This is best understood when you move your thumb alongside your finger. Play with this idea for a moment until it becomes clear and you understand why you tack on a header.

When you first begin sailing upwind, always watch what the wind is doing and try to predict what will happen next. Mentally time the wind shifts. If they're small shifts and less than a minute apart, don't tack on the headers, because the header you've been sailing in will soon become a lift. Meanwhile, always head up in the lifts as they come; over time the lifts and headers in this unsteady air will generally average out. If you do tack in this situation, it's possible that you'll find yourself headed again before gaining any real speed on the new tack. When the shifts are a few minutes apart noticeably changing your course, tack on the headers and sail on the lifted tack to your advantage.

For example, as my crew and I sailed to windward in my Potter, a Ranger 23 crossed our bow and tacked on top of us. We tacked away looking for better wind. As the wind shifted we headed up, finding ourselves on the lifted tack. The skipper of the Ranger 23, now sailing on a header, failed to notice. We tacked on the next header, and sailed on that lift, easily crossing in front of the Ranger. The never to be forgotten expression on the skipper's face was one of complete disbelief as we popped out from behind that Ranger's jib. How could a Potter with two people in it out sail the faster Ranger? Actually we didn't, but sailing the lifted tacks shortened our course considerably and that made all the difference.

Telltales, a Tool of Sail Trim

   Relative telltales are used to find wind direction, and serve as guides when sailing by the wind. These telltales, or tells as they are known, are pieces of yarn attached to your shrouds with tape. Position your tells on the shrouds so they're easy to see.

   Another relative tell is the masthead fly.

. Below its wind direction arrow, at the top of the mast, are two tabs on rods. These tabs are adjusted so they're right under the arrow when your Potter is beating. When tuning the Potter, the masthead fly is positioned right over the leeward tab. Then starting with the jib, the sails are shaped and trimmed for wind and water conditions to give proper helm balance. The masthead fly always let's you know how well you're pointing and serves as a benchmark for all sail adjustments when beating.

Telltales for Sails

As you sail, you're not just using relative tells. Your
sails should also be equipped with tells that show

how the air flows over them. You'll need that information before you can trim sails effectively.

If you don't have tells on your sails, put them on. You can use dark colored yarn or spinnaker cloth. Yarn is easy to use. Just thread it on a sail needle, and push it through the sail where you need the tell. Tie a stopper knot in the yarn close to each side of the sail and trim off any excess yarn beyond six inches.

If you choose spinnaker cloth for your tells, they can be purchased in kit form at the boat store. When using spinnaker cloth, place the starboard tells a few inches above the port tells. This makes reading them easier when using the lee tell. Whichever of the two different tells you choose, each have their disadvantages. Yarn can snag on the sail stitching, or when wet, become temporarily ineffective. Spinnaker cloth, after prolonged sun exposure curls up, which ends its usefulness. However, like most of your equipment, it must be maintained to be effective.

Locations for Tells

The jib will need three tells on each side. Place the tells about eighteen inches aft of the luff. Put the first tell half way between the tack and the head of the sail. The other two are located halfway from the center tell toward the tack and head of the sail.

The mainsail will also need three tells on each side. These are located two feet aft of the luff because of disturbed air flow around the mast. Position them the same as you did for the jib. Also, put three tells on the leech of the sail located below each batten.

Reading Telltales

As the air splits the luff of the jib, it moves slower along the windward side, than on the lee side of the sail. Looking through the sail, when the sun isn't shinning directly on it, you can see that the tells on the lee side are more active. While watching them, you'll also notice that they occasionally move in opposite directions during wind shifts. For instance, if you luff up, the windward tell will lift, while the lee tell drops. Just the opposite happens when you bear away from the wind.

To sort this all out, the windward tells will show what you're doing wrong. They're lifting, showing that you're sailing too high, or close to the wind as you luff up. The leeward tell shows what you need to do. When it drops, you head down, away from the wind. As you comply, both tells fly horizontally again. It's best to commit something like this to memory, rather than try to figure it out as you go along. Even with experience, you can get confused watching the tells when the wind is difficult and the tells seem to go crazy. If that happens, just refer back to the mast head fly or the tells on the shrouds and you'll quickly solve the problem.

When using the tells, the object is to always have both windward and leeward tells stream horizontally. Because your sails are set so the tells stream level as you beat to windward, use your tiller to keep them flowing that way, heading up in the lifts and down in the headers. This is called sailing by the wind.

However, when sailing in light shifty air, it's sometimes quicker to adjust the sails to the wind shifts rather than waiting for the boat to respond. This will keep your boat moving faster. When reaching, as I mentioned before, the windward tells won't work in the lee of the jib stay. Watch only the lee tells in this situation. When running, the tells stream in all directions as you sail dead downwind. This is because the wind is perpendicular to the sail and takes the path of least resistance around it. The tells on the shrouds aren't reliable in this situation due to the air flowing off the mainsail. Watch the masthead fly; it gives the best information on wind direction when sailing downwind. When you can, head up slightly to make the tells flow across the sails. There's a slight advantage in speed, but it also increases the distance to your downwind destination.

The tells along the leech of the mainsail show how much tension is needed on the leech.

If the leech of the sail has too much tension, it will be closed and the air on its lee side won't exit properly. When that happens, the tells will disappear from sight to leeward of the sail. Ease your mainsheet first, then your vang if necessary to correct this. To set the leech tension correctly when all the tells are flowing, pull in on the vang until the top tell just breaks momentarily from its consistent flow.

You may have wondered why you need more than one tell along the luffs and leeches of your sails. The three tells give a better overall indication of the sail's twist from top to bottom, and provide information needed for setting the barber haulers and vang. The more information you have to work with, the easier it will be to trim your sails effectively.

Using Telltales

Always watch the tells as you trim the sail. When you fine tune your sail, use small adjustments to the sheet until the lee tells on the sail flutter faster. This is very important. Even easing the sheet an eighth of an inch will make a difference. The faster the air moves over the lee side of the sail, the more power it has. When you can see them, use your lee tells to sail by. They're in faster air and more sensitive to change.

Sail Trim

Sail trim, a part of helmsmanship, goes far beyond just pulling in the sheets when the sails begins to luff. Every corner of a sail is trimmed when conditions change. It's these corners, the head, tack, and clew, that change the shape and fullness of the sail making it more efficient. The Cunningham, vang, and outhaul are the tools used for the mainsail. The halyard, barber hauler, and sheet are the tools used for the jib. As you become more familiar with the shaping of sails as a part of sail trim, your sailing performance will improve.

Shaping Sails

This is the more difficult part of sail trim. There are no indicators for this other than books or examples left by more experienced sailors who've taken the time to show us the way. Generally, as you shape the sails, you're trying to do one of two things, either power the sails up or down.

To make those changes effectively you need to understand the difference between camber and draft. Using any mainsail, draft is measured from the boom to the maximum fullness of the sail. Camber, the curve a sail takes between it's luff and leech, is measured from the mast aft to the deepest part of its curve.

A mainsail's draft is controlled from the outhaul at the end of the boom. The Cunningham at the mast moves the camber (deepest part of the curve) forward or releases it aft to change the shape of the sail. A jibs draft is adjusted with its sheet. Its camber is shifted by adjusting the sheet lead with the barber hauler and by changing jib halyard tension. Both draft and camber work together to provide the sail shape needed for particular wind and water conditions.

To point well in flat water the camber in both sails on a sloop is located aft, almost fifty percent back from the luff. When the camber is moved forward, the sails will have more power. This translates to more speed, but less pointing ability. However, when sailing on the wind, the real art of shaping sails demands that you shift the camber just enough to gain the best of both speed and pointing ability.

An Outline of Potter Sail Trim

This outline will be your benchmark for learning about trimming sails and balancing your Potter. Take this information out on the water with you and use it.

A simple way to begin learning sail trim is to get out a pencil and paper and copy the outline down. This idea probably seems ridiculous considering today's existing technology, but this effort will enhance your ability to understand and retain its content. When you finish, you'll be more familiar with the outline and have a copy of it. Take your copy sailing and keep it on the bunk where you can refer to it often.

As you look at the outline, you'll see that it's organized by wind velocity and points of sail. Before you attempt to learn this outline, first check how the draft in the sails relate to the three different wind speeds in the outline.

In very light winds, category one, less than medium draft is used. Medium to slightly more draft is used in category two winds. Draft is reduced in heavier category three winds. Knowing this ahead of time gives a general idea of what's happening throughout the outline for low, medium, and high wind felocities.

Keep in mind that this outline of sail trim, which is very valuable as a place to start, is just a model. It does have it's limitations. The biggest of those is that it's easy for a beginning learner to assume that all you have to do is set the sails for each category. That's just what I did. It's good for a start, but experience shows that you must make minor trim adjustments as the wind increases, all along the way from zero to six knots in the first category. Then six knots seamlessly flows into seven knots which is the beginning of the second category. Because you already know how draft is used in the outline, you can see where this is headed. Just remember, wherever you're sailing in the outline, adjustments are always done in small increments just to meet changing conditions.

For example, the skipper thinks there's a problem with weather helm.

"First I'll lift the centerboard a little. That seems to help, but not enough. Better tension the

Cunningham. That will open the leech more. There, that's the way it should be. The helm has a much better feel. That's just what I want!"

Remember, sail trim is an art form. There are no absolutes.

After some study and time on the water you'll begin to develop what works. As that happens, you'll smile, and realize how much fun this is. You probably already know that you'll continue to sail for many years into the future, so take this learning opportunity and make the most of it.

Ask yourself what kind of sailing you'll be doing three years from now. Will it be the same old stuff, or will you blow the socks off those skippers who thought you were just an easy mark?

Light Winds   0 - 6 Knots

A. Beating

1. Mainsail
a. less than medium draft, Cunningham off

b. light tension on halyard and sheet

c. leech open, tells flowing

d. vang slack,

2. Jib
a. Inboard barber hauler slightly on for more draft, tells flowing

b. light tension on halyard

c. light sheet tension, leech parallel to lee side of the main

3. Balance
a. centerboard full down

b. rudder blade needs more aft rake if lee helm

c. heel boat to shape sails, reduce wetted

surface, and lee helm

B. Reaching

1. Mainsail

    a. full draft unless very light, Cunningham off

    b. slight vang tension, unless very light, top tell

       just breaking

    c. head up in lulls and down in gusts

2. Jib

    a. Outboard barber hauler on with sheet at cabin

       top level, lee tells horizontal

    b. tension halyard to increase draft and forward

       mast rake

3. Balance

    a. centerboard half up, when lee helm lower

       board, weather helm, raise board

    b. heel boat to keep sails full and help balance

       helm, keep weight forward, avoid transom drag

C. Running

1. Mainsail
a. flatten, less than moderate draft

b. Cunningham off

c. keep top batten parallel to boom with vang

d. head up in lulls and down in gusts

2. Jib
a. wing out jib

b. outboard barber hauler down to deck

c. foot and leech taught

d. jib perpendicular to center line of boat

3. Balance
a. mast rake, use jib halyard tension to pull mast forward

b. centerboard full up, heel to steer, avoid rudder use

c. weight forward, avoid transom drag

Medium Winds   7 - 15 Knot

A. Beating - powering up

   1. Mainsail

      a. increase draft with outhaul

      b. camber aft for pointing, Cunningham off

      c. increase luff tension as needed

      d. Sheet harder, upper tell on leech just breaking

   2. Jib

      a. inboard barber hauler on, tells horizontal, increase sheet tension

      b. leech parallels curve of lee side of main

   3. Balance

      a. if weather helm, lift board slightly, Cunningham on, decrease draft, ease vang, then sheet as needed

      b. sail boat at ten degrees heel or less

B. Reaching

   1. Mainsail

a. Cunningham off

b. full draft in mainsail with outhaul

c. vang on, top tell on leech just breaking

2. Jib

a. outboard barber hauler on, sheet to cabin top level

b. lee tells horizontal, use constant sheet adjustment

3. Balance

a. lift board until slight weather helm

b. slight heel to minimize wetted surface

c. weight forward for reduced transom drag

C. Running

1. Mainsail

a. flatten with outhaul, maximum projected area needed

b. Cunningham off

c. vang, top batten parallel to boom

d. use masthead fly to sail by

2. Jib

  a. pole out, trim flat

  b. outboard barber hauler on, jib sheet at deck level

3. Balance

  a. centerboard up, use heel to steer, avoid rudder movement

  b. weight forward, avoid transom drag

Heavy Winds 16 Knots and Up

A. Beating - powering down

1. Mainsail

  a. use outhaul, flatten sail

  b. pull camber forward with Cunningham to open leech

  c. ease vang to twist off top of sail and reduce heel if needed

  d. ease sheet to reduce weather helm

  e. reef when needed

2. Jib

    a. as you tack, tension halyard to move camber forward

    b. barber haulers off, twists off top of jib, and opens slot for

    main when eased due to helm

    c. sheet jib harder.

3. Balance

    a. lift centerboard about six inches, rudder blade full forward

    b. ease main when necessary, sail boat almost flat

    c. if needed, carry luff in main for control

B. Reaching

1.Mainsail

    a. keep same setting as beating

    b. ease mainsheet in gusts, keep boat on its feet, don't lose control, head off in gusts, head up in lulls

c. use vang to control upper sail twist

2. Jib

   a. keep same settings as beating

   b. outboard barber hauler off for upper sail twist if needed

3. Balance

   a. raise board enough to balance helm

C. Running

1. Mainsail

   a. flat main, full tension on outhaul, Cunningham off

   b. full vang, no twist off, it causes rolling

   c. keep top batten parallel to boom

   d. sheet main in to project less sail area if loosing control

2. Jib

   a. pull sheet to deck with barber hauler

   b. wing out sail, use a pole if you can

   c. tension halyard if jib begins to pump

3. Balance

    a. move aft for better steering control

    b. let board part way down unless waves, play the waves

    c. careful steering is critical for control

Special Exceptions for Sail Trim

Sails are trimmed differently for other special conditions. If you've been sailing inside a sheltered harbor in moderate winds, but are now passing the breakwater and entering the bay, your sails will have to be trimmed to keep the boat moving through the waves generated on the open bay. Waves are a special challenge, especially when the wind is light. First, increase twist in the tops of your sails to minimize stall created by a pitching mast. Ease both your jib and main sheets slightly. Increase sail draft to keep your speed up. Pointing is not the issue when beating in these conditions, speed is needed to maintain steering control and reduce leeway. Using the barber hauler, shift the jib's camber slightly forward for more power, but keep twist in the upper part of the jib. Having the camber forward in the jib will help keep air flow attached to the lee side of the sails providing more power.

When the wind is shifty and gusty, sails need to be trimmed differently. This could be caused by a coming storm front or, you could just be sailing with a lot of other boats that are disrupting the wind. Your telltales will show this. The masthead fly will not line up with the tells on the shrouds and the tells on the sails will be very unsteady, moving up and down while lifting off the surface of the sails. The best you can do in these conditions is to trim for as much of this shifty wind as possible.

The best approach is to keep your Potter's rig flexible. Ease your jib and main slightly. Twist off the tops of your sails, not only to stabilize the boat when heeling, but to trim the sails to best effect with the upper wind direction that's different from wind near the water. The object is to trim effectively for as much of this wind as you can.

Sails

Next to the wind for making a Potter go, sails are your boat's most important asset. As your helmsmanship and sail trimming skills continue to improve, you'll spend lots of time looking at sails, becoming more aware about how they set.

If you were racing in a competitive one design fleet, your sails would need replacing about every three or four years. However, those of us who are trailer sailing often keep our sails much longer. If your sails are not too old, they can be repaired. Such things as holes in a sail, torn batten pockets, or a fluttering leech can all be fixed. However, you should balance the cost of repairs and the age of your sails against the price of new ones. For example, you've been using your sails twice a month for five years. You have a torn batten pocket, several of the sail slugs will need replacing. Using a conservative point of view the life left in those sails is about twenty-four months at best. Investing much money in repairs may not be the best idea. Old sails stretch out, losing their shape and become very discouraging to use. Putting new sails on your boat is like putting a new engine in an old car, making it fun to drive again.

If you decide to buy new sails, do your homework. If there are other Potters around, look at their sails to see if there's anything you like. If not, call International Marine, and ask about the sails they sell with their new Potters. When you do see sails you like, find out who made them, and contact the sailmaker for a price. Buying sails on the cheap is not a good idea. Remember, you'll probably have to live with those sails for a long time. It's very discouraging to use sails you're not pleased with, especially when you've put so much time into learning sail trim. These days, some of the less expensive sails are outsourced and mass produced. You can save money with these, but you must take what they give you. Any extras you'll need may have to be done somewhere else adding to their original cost.

Most skippers who want more sail area for their Potters use larger head sails. The lapper, the next size up from the working jib, is very popular because it's adaptable to a variety of wind conditions and points well. The larger genoa has not been as successful on Potters when beating. This is mostly due to their poor sheeting angle. It's more work to use, and requires very long whisker poles when going downwind.

Using larger sails doesn't always make a Potter a better boat. I've spent years answering the question, "How fast will a Potter go?" One possible answer was using larger sails. Custom sails were made. Once on the boat, they did make a difference. However, when the wind increased those sails became a real handful and not much fun to use. It soon became obvious that I needed to re-think how I wanted to answer the "how fast" question. Today, Ah Tiller the Fun uses a standard suit of sails with the small jib. The boat is much more fun to sail, and when it's important to go fast, it's helmsmanship and sail trim that get me there. I've been just as successful with the smaller sails as I was with the larger ones. Having smaller sails has forced me to learn better sail trim.

It's said that even world class sailors are only able to access about eighty-five percent of their sails' efficiency. So long as you can access more efficiency using better sail trim than those around you, you'll do well when it comes to performance.

Before buying larger sails, consider how you're using the boat. If your significant other is sailing with you, or you lack experience, then the working jib and standard main will do just fine.

Because Potters carry what is known as a three quarter rig, their main source of power comes from the mainsail. Even when the wind is very light, and that big jib hangs like a curtain, it's the mainsail that continues to move the boat.

Sailing Alternatives

It's always a good idea to modify a Potter to fit your sailing needs. Motivation for doing this might come from sailing with a significant other who is nervous about heeling. It could be that you're recovering from an illness or injury, or maybe you're just getting old. These are all good reasons to make your Potter more comfortable and easier to sail.

This reminds me of a story I heard awhile back. A husband and wife were sailing their P15. As the Potter sailed along it was quite gusty which made sailing difficult, taking the husband's full attention just to manage the boat. The wife sat there very quietly just hanging on until she had enough. "Thomas," she said, "Make it stop." And he did.

I sail with a lot of old guys, I'm one myself. When I race, it usually takes me a day just to recover. It's probably also the same for other older skippers. Although this is limiting, it's not a reason to stop sailing. So what can we do as we get older, but still want to get out on the water?

Potter Ergonomics

How do we make our Potters easier to sail? This was a question I wanted to answer while sailing my own boat.

A Potter can be divided into systems that make the boat go. Starting with the worst systems, I began to redesign them to be more efficient, simpler, and easier to use. One example of this was inside sheeting for the jib. Each system had to operate smoothly in all conditions. In time, all the systems became much easier to operate, making the boat a lot more fun to sail.

Reducing Sail

If you're facing physical limitations, an important step would be to reduce sail area. Using a smaller jib would be a simple way to do that. Tacking would be easier, especially with inside sheeting. Another approach would be to leave the jib on deck and only use it off the wind like you might with a spinnaker. You could choose to leave the jib at home, not using it at all. There isn't any rule that says you have to sail with one. The Potter sails fine without a jib; just pull the centerboard up a little to balance the helm.

Choosing one of those options would make your sailing life easier and probably save on rigging time. Other possibilities also come to mind. You can always take a crew to help out, or you can choose a completely different rig for your Potter, one that will be easier to use. Whichever you choose, have fun doing it. That's what real pottering is all about.

The Lateen Rig

If you're looking for a boat that's easier to handle, your sloop rig could be replaced with the lateen rig. A Sunfish rig has been successfully used on Potters for a long time. Several skippers I sail with have done that. They rig their boats in half the time it used to take. The mast is unstayed and slides into a tube which comes up through the cabin top just forward of the standard mast location. The lateen mast is much shorter than the sloop version, and can be stepped from alongside the boat. Once the mast is stepped, the boom and yard are connected to it. The halyard is then fastened to the yard and a downhaul on the boom tensions the sail acting as a vang. The only other lines that need attention when sailing are the halyard and sheet. Because the lateen sail extends forward of the mast it's easier to jibe and sheet in.

Potters sail well with this rig. In very light air the
lateen Potters can lead the fleet. The sloop rigged
Potters however, are slightly faster when the wind

comes up making their jibs more effective. When considering the advantages of the lateen rig, those skippers who use it are willing to exchange the difference in speed for the convenience of the rig.

A Potter Picnic Boat

Some years back, when I bought my boat, there was a picture of a Potter in the office of International Marine. The skipper in the picture was standing in the cockpit with a remote control device in his hand. At the bow of his Potter was a model tug boat working hard to tow him along through a calm. The picture made quite a statement, leading me to believe that with some imagination almost anything might be possible with a Potter.

While daydreaming, I began to think about using the Potter as a picnic boat. The more I thought about it, the better I liked the idea. I had mental visions of a family headed for their favorite cove. Their Potter was cluttered with sand pails, shovels, a beach umbrella, towels, and of course, the kids. Several air mattresses tied to the boat followed along in the Potter's wake. The scene looked delightful. Further visions showed an elderly couple cruising the edge of a marsh enjoying their lunch while birdwatching. The possibilities for using a Potter seemed endless.

Potters make excellent small motor boats. They are very seaworthy for their size, and have little impact on the environment or your expenses. The cabin provides good shelter, and its self bailing cockpit is easier to keep clean after being at the beach all day than the bilges of an open skiff would be. A Potter, when under power, is more comfortable to operate than a skiff of the same size. Using a rudder makes steering easier, not having to turn the whole motor and allows you to sit forward in the lee of the cabin away from the noise. The centerboard provides stability and helps the boat track better in the wind. The Potter is more maneuverable than other small motor boats at slower speeds because of its centerboard. It's true that the Potter only goes about four knots, but at that speed it will cover about seven or eight miles of shoreline in a few hours. It will be easy to explore new areas using different launching ramps if over the water distances become an obstacle to time.

The picnic Potter would be ideal for those who love getting out on the water, but find rigging and sailing have become too demanding. Think of those sunset cruises, an amber sky, the lights just coming on along the waterfront in the evening. Imagine only spending ten minutes for launching and less than a gallon of gas for a full day's worth of adventure.

A Gentle Way to Sail

As you remember a while back in the introduction, there was a person taking a break relaxing and observing the activities of others out on the water. Wondering what life on the water might be like, he wandered out onto the dock. Since then, time has passed, leaving him with many experiences. Let's join with him now as his story comes to a conclusion.

It's been a long time since he took that first step into a Potter when he wandered down onto the dock.

Since that time he's had new adventures on the water learning to sail. And by joining with others he's now become an excepted part of the local sailing community. Now his enthusiasm has increased to the point that just the thought of walking down onto the dock spending the day sailing is exhilarating. It's taken some serious effort, but he's completed what has been for him a long path toward becoming the owner and skipper his own Potter.

One of the most amazing parts of this process was the discovery of the Potter. There he was, just walking along that dock past so many different types of small boats. Not knowing anything about them, he stopped in front of one, paused for a moment, then just stepped aboard because it felt right. Later, as he came to know more about boats, he discovered the choice he'd made that day was the right one.

So here he is, finally standing on a dock next to his own Potter anticipating his first solo sail.

This is a special moment that will not be forgotten. He's worked hard to make this sailing dream happen with the extra money for the boat and the sailing lessons. His view from the water will now be a very different one from that of walking along the shoreline as he did in the past.

The motor idles quietly, like the lady she is, his Potter waits patiently, a halyard rattles slightly against the mast in the gentle breeze bringing his attention back to the lines in his hand, but still, once again, he takes just one more moment before stepping aboard and changing his life from what it once was, into the one he's dreamed of for so very long.

Glossary

athwart ship: from one side of the boat to the other.

bend on: to attach sails to spars or stays.

blocks: pulleys used for tackles to handle heavy loads.

bridge deck: the deck connecting the footwell to the cabin.

bunt: The part of a reefed mainsail hanging under the boom.

camber: the position of the draft of a sail fore or aft.

cat's paws: ruffled patches of water showing where the wind is.

clew of sail: the lower rear corner of a jib or mainsail.

combing: the rail around the cockpit to keep the water out.

compression post: vertical post in the cabin to support the mast.

Cunningham: used to tension the luff, changing the sails camber.

ebb tide: the current flows toward the sea, lowering the water.

fairlead: determines the lead of the jib sheet to its cam cleat.

fenders: placed along the hull to protect the boat from damage.

flood tide: the water rises as the current flows in from the sea.

foot of sail: the bottom of the sail between the tack and clew.

four fall tackle: a line rove through two double blocks.

furled: a sail that is rolled into its self and tied with sail gaskets.

gooseneck: attaches the boom to the mast.

grounding: sailing the boat ashore.

harbor furl: sail neatly furled with no ends or lines hanging out.

head of a sail: upper corner of a sail where the halyard attaches.

header: wind that forces your course away from its destination.

helm: the tiller or wheel used for steering a boat

hiking stick: an extension for the tiller.

hiking strap: a strap to tuck your foot under when sitting on the rail.

knots: wind or boat speed in nautical miles per hour.

lateen rig: a triangular sail set on spars at a forty-five degree angle to the mast.

leech: the aft edge of a sail.

lift: wind direction allowing you to sail closer to your destination.

lines: rope used for running rigging such as sheets or halyards.

luff: the leading edge of the sail.

pinching: sailing too close to the wind.

plotting waypoints: using longitude and latitude from a chart for entering plots into a GPS.

points of sail: beating, reaching, and running.

rigging tangs: normally used to attach stays or shrouds to a mast.

roach: sail aft of a straight line between the clew and head of the mainsail.

sculling: using a single oar from the stern to move the boat.

sheets: the lines that control the sails.

shrouds: standing rigging to support the mast from the sides of the boat.

spreaders: small spars that push the shrouds out away from the mast to better support it.

stays: standing rigging providing fore and aft support for the mast.

stopper knot: a figure eight knot stopping the line from running through a block.

tack of the sail: the forward lower corner of the sail.

topping lift: the line that holds the boom up when the sail is down.

trailer tongue: the receiver on the trailer that goes over the ball hitch.

trimmed: when a sail is adjusted closely to the wind.

twist: allowing the upper part of the mainsail to twist to leeward.

vang: a tackle to hold the boom down and control mainsail leech tension.

wheel jack: the jack to lift the trailer tongue.